. . . and for Yale

It took a return from San Francisco for sufficient time to read and reflect on (your book). I was amused in places, surprised in others, and moved throughout. . . .While I had known you as the very best of volunteer Yale men, there were few aspects of your life that I had discovered before. . . . a well-wrought memoir.

Don Lamm, Yale Class of 1953
Former CEO, WW Norton & Company

Your book . . . is warm-hearted and wonderful and appeals to me on many levels and should appeal to a broad audience as well.

The parts where you describe your own process of engaging with Yale at all stages, from young adult to present day life, are powerful and eloquent in their positive and hopeful message and re-creation of thoughts and feelings, and actions and motivations, as you went through undergrad life. You also bring to life and give flesh to the meaning of friendship in all things and endeavors. . .

I feel sure that anyone who is interested in Yale from the standpoint of applicant or relative of an applicant would want to read this book . . . It is also a book for alumni who may want to relive or come to grips with their own experiences or expand their participation in Yale activities going forward.

Warren Rothman, Yale Class of 1965
Lawyer, Business Consultant, Author

What a delight . . . Your descriptions took me back to a time and place deeply familiar, but they also helped me see it in a new light. Equally important, your observations linked our experience to today's university and the ongoing work of educating young women and men. . . . So thank you for being so observant, for sharing your love affair with Yale with the rest of us, and for letting me read it!

Mick Smyer, Yale Class of 1972
Provost, Bucknell University

Kirk Casselman has long been a dedicated, loyal and hard-working volunteer for Yale. He represents the devotion of the kind we hope to stimulate in all alumni, but that gets expressed in many decades of service by only a few.

Jeffrey Brenzel, Yale Class of 1975
Master of Timothy Dwight College
Former Dean of Undergraduate Admissions
Former Executive Director of the Association of Yale Alumni

. . . and for Yale

Why Bright College Years Never Fade Away

J. Kirk Casselman

iUniverse LLC
Bloomington

. . . AND FOR YALE
WHY BRIGHT COLLEGE YEARS NEVER FADE AWAY

iUniverse books may be ordered through booksellers or by contacting:

iUniverse
1663 Liberty Drive
Bloomington, IN 47403
www.iuniverse.com
1-800-Authors (1-800-288-4677)

ISBN: 978-1-4759-9339-4 (sc)
ISBN: 978-1-4759-9341-7 (hc)
ISBN: 978-1-4759-9340-0 (e)

Library of Congress Control Number: 2013909957

Printed in the United States of America.

iUniverse rev. date: 7/12/2013

Table of Contents

Preface vii

Introduction. xi

Chapter 1 – Admission to Yale 1

Chapter 2 – Preparation. 5

Chapter 3 – Arriving for the First Time. 15

Chapter 4 – Academics 29

Chapter 5 – Athletics 37

Chapter 6 – Music and Other Activities. 43

Chapter 7 – Fraternities 47

Chapter 8 – Senior Societies. 51

Chapter 9 – Junior Year – On the Way Down. 59

Chapter 10 – Junior Year – The Utter Nadir 61

Chapter 11 – Junior Year – Headed Back Up 65

Chapter 12 – Summer in France 71

Chapter 13 – Senior Year 75

Chapter 14 – Law School 81

Chapter 15 – Alumni Schools Committee. 85

Chapter 16 – The Yale Club of San Francisco 93

Chapter 17 – The Association of Yale Alumni 97

Chapter 18 – Community Service Summer Fellowship 103

Chapter 19 – Yale Day of Service 109

Chapter 20 – Bulldogs Across America 111

Chapter 21 – Yale Career Network 117

Chapter 22 – Music Program for Graduates. 121

Chapter 23 – YaleGALE 123

Chapter 24 – Reunions 127

Chapter 25 – Reunion at the White House 135

Chapter 26 – In Summation 143

Epilogue. 147

Preface

T his is a book about Yale and me. The diligent reader will find factual errors in this book but that doesn't matter. This book is not intended to be a factually accurate history of either my life or Yale. Rather, it is intended to be a subjective, perhaps even impressionistic, view of my association with Yale and its institutions and traditions and the effect they have had on my life.

Why do it?

Why subject myself to the agonies of writing a book, especially a book about myself, revealing things perhaps better left unsaid? This exercise will be an internal exploration of my past, an attempt to set in perspective aspects of my life that are currently disjointed. Second, and more importantly, it will serve to inform future applicants to Yale about the wondrous aspects of that great institution and the incredible influence it has on its graduates. It may help students, therefore, in making informed judgments about where they apply to college and why, a goal I have pursued for decades.

It was reported in the popular press in early 2013 that high school students from low-income families do not think about applying to the top colleges even though they may have earned top grades and test scores. These findings, by educational researchers at Stanford and Harvard, resulted from students not knowing how much financial aid is available at top schools and from students not knowing anybody who went to top schools. This book should help to rectify both situations.

I do not write this book to tell all, since doing so would do no one any real good—not Yale, myself or others mentioned in this book. Rather, my intention is to bust myths about Yale and to tell as much as is necessary to provide future matriculants with information to apply confidently and meaningfully to Yale. Oh, and we'll discuss whether this material will be on the exam.

Among other things, prefaces are for acknowledging others, usually those who have inspired the author or those who have helped in producing the work. Following this practice, I acknowledge, in particular, Calvin Trillin '57 and S.J. Perlman, both of whom exhibit for me the kind of love of language and joy in writing that lies nascent within me and which I hope to liberate in writing this book.

I also wish to acknowledge Ellis Kaplan, Harvard educated architect and writer whose early suggestion prompted this book, Aaron C.F. Finkbiner III, who provided the working title, Stuart Odell, whose encouragement has always been inspirational, Roger Clapp '68, who gave focus to this effort with his question ("We all loved Yale. Why did some of us do more than others for Yale after graduation?"), Hampton Sides '84, who, when asked for advice on the one thing a neophyte writer should know before undertaking the writing of a book, replied, "Have your head examined," Don Lamm '53, whose wise professional counsel guided every step of this project, and, of course, my dear wife Louise, who has tolerated, indeed encouraged, my passions since senior year at Yale.

J. Kirk Casselman
Santa Fe, New Mexico
February 2013

Introduction

Bright College Years

Bright college years, with pleasure rife,
The shortest, gladdest years of life;
How swiftly are ye gliding by!
Oh, why doth time so quickly fly?
The seasons come, the seasons go,
The earth is green or white with snow,
But time and change shall naught avail
To break the friendships formed at Yale.

In after years, should troubles rise
To cloud the blue of sunny skies,
How bright will seem, through mem'ry's haze
Those happy, golden, bygone days!
Oh, let us strive that ever we
May let these words our watch-cry be,
Where'er upon life's sea we sail:
"For God, for Country and for Yale!"

Alma Mater of Yale University
Words by H. S. Durand, Class of 1881
Music by Carl Wilhelm

Yale University is the third oldest university in the United States. It was founded in 1701 in what was then the Colony of Connecticut. Its 1,100 faculty teach 5,300 undergraduates and

6,100 graduate and professional students. Yale's commitment to undergraduate education is rare among research universities of its caliber. Its endowment was valued in 2011 at $19.4 billion making it the second largest of any academic institution worldwide.

Apart from these cold facts, what's it like to be an undergraduate at Yale?

Every year, thousands upon thousands of college-bound students ask themselves this question. For decades in the early part of the last century, the best-known writing that sought to answer this question was *Stover at Yale,* which chronicled the exploits of a fictional undergraduate, Dink Stover.

One hundred years have passed since 1912 when Owen Johnson first published *Stover at Yale.* About half that number of years have passed since Kingman Brewster, Jr., then President of Yale University, in 1968 wrote his introduction to Johnson's book. 1968 was also the year I was graduated from Yale and was about to begin my work with young people aspiring to attend Yale and with Yale undergraduates enjoying "the shortest, gladdest years of life."

In the pages that follow, I will attempt to give the reader a somewhat more current description of life at Yale. I do so with the expectation that future applicants will be able to make more informed judgments about applying to Yale. In addition, I have dedicated considerable space to the discussion of alumni activities with the intent of letting applicants know that the Yale experience can last a lifetime. I hope this discussion will be of interest to alumni and other readers who will develop a deeper understanding of Yale University and perhaps relive, or come to grips with, their own experiences or expand their participation in Yale activities going forward.

In his introduction, Brewster pointed out that, despite the difference in argot between Stover's Yale and the then current Yale, the pattern of the Yale experience was the same: "Self-conscious confidence to the point of arrogance enshrouded the young man as he entered Phelps Gateway. Self-doubt festered into self-pity as he found that not all his assumptions about himself and his Yale world were beyond question . . . (Self-pity is followed by) rediscovery, and finally to mature ambition." These five stages–self-conscious confidence, self-doubt, self-pity, rediscovery and mature ambition–provide structure for the narrative that follows in the early chapters of this book.

On the other hand, Brewster also pointed out that, in his era, "the openness of invitation to the struggle of all against all for campus success" was essentially more a measure of effort and accomplishment and contribution to Yale than it was to inherited status. In this regard, Brewster argued, the pattern of life for Yale undergraduates was a "democracy", yet the meaning of that term was quite different in 1968 than it was in 1912. The open competition in Stover's time for "corporately defined success" as a standard has been replaced by an "individualistic, almost anarchistic, definition of democracy".

In the years since 1968, in working with applicants and with undergraduates, I have observed that the pattern of life at Yale has remained essentially the same. In Brewster's terms, "College as a place to 'find' yourself, then as now, requires teachers, administrative mentors, and especially parents to take the terrible risk of letting students get 'lost'." This process of maturation is now open to a much greater range of students as a result of many decades of aggressive diversification of the undergraduate student body at Yale.

That diversification began in earnest with a letter written by Kingman Brewster and addressed to John Muyskens, then Director of Admissions, dated March 15, 1967. In it, President Brewster summarized Yale's admissions policy, giving relative weight to intellectual capacity, placing a broad construction on the definition of leadership, identifying moral concern as a specific consideration in the admissions process and affirming Yale's interest in qualified sons and daughters of alumni.

More specifically, Brewster wrote, "I do think that where social and economic and racial circumstance has made the testable strengths difficult to assess fairly, it is desirable to go as far as possible to uncover other evidence which might bear witness to special potentialities. The standard of admissibility certainly should not be lower for the disadvantaged, but the best evidence of capacity may lie outside the conventional records." Moreover, he said, "An excessively homogeneous class will not learn anywhere near as much from each other as a class whose backgrounds and interests and values have something new to contribute to the common experience."

In the belief that the fullest understanding of the Yale experience will come from matching the historical roots of its institutions with their current embodiment, at least as I have lived with them, I have introduced the early chapters of this book with quotations from Johnson's book appropriate to my own narrative.

No introduction to the Yale experience would be complete without citing my classmate Dick Brodhead, former Dean of Yale College and now president of Duke University, in his welcoming speech to the freshman class of 2002 entitled *The Way to Worry*.

Brodhead revealed that Yale graduates ten, twenty, thirty, even fifty years out wanted to confess some undetected college sin that had gnawed at them for years. "I probably just got in because I came from the area." "I probably just got in because I came from a remote area." "I went to a school with a lot of advantages, and I was probably admitted of the strength of those advantages, not my own attributes." "I went to school with no advantages; I could never have been the equal of those people who went to really good schools." "I was just an athlete." "I was just an intellectual."

To which Brodhead responded:

> What low opinion do you have of your university, what level of incompetence do you attribute to us, that we would admit 1,300 students each by separate act of mistake? . . . You are in fact the very person we wanted to come here, the one we chose in place of many others . . . We seek students endowed with a whole range of human gifts who share the

drive to develop their gifts to the fullest extent, for their own pleasure and for the good of others; and we count on our students not just to be adequate to the demands of this place but to enrich its life, to help make it happen.

. . . If you are nervous on entering Yale . . . remember . . . (t)o worry is just human . . . Anxiety is the experience in negative form of the same energy that is positively experienced as excitement . . . Let me coach you in some right and wrong ways to worry . . . While failure is the obvious thing to fear, the reality is that you have far more to fear from your addiction to success . . . I worry that your desire to be thought a success might tempt you to try only those things at Yale at which you are already confident of succeeding . . . Are you confident there is any subject you will be content to be ignorant of for the rest of your life? I promise you that no one will say of you when you are forty: "He is strangely ignorant, but I hear he got good grades at Yale."

I implore you not to let anxiety turn your social life into a social self-enclosure . . . Your classmates will be among your great teachers . . . To the extent that you shut yourself in from the whole community, you will deprive yourself of the testing and enrichment that others could have given you—and deprive them of the education you could have given them in return.

But I have rarely met a student who thought to worry about the one thing that would strike me as really worth worrying about at this point in your career: coming up with some answer to the questions, What is an education and how am I to get one? . . . Your education is an ongoing process, one that is fed in a hundred ways and never to be completed, by which you win the ability to understand the world in its multitudinous dimensions and to act in the world in a reflective, constructive way . . .

We didn't accept you because you got good grades and racked up long lists of accomplishments in high school; nor have we brought you here to perform those feats again. We picked you because we judged you to have the aptitude to lead a thoughtful and constructive life; and we brought you here to help you prepare your powers . . . You will advance on this goal if you seek out every new domain of knowledge and every challenge that can be posed to your achieved understanding–if you stay, that is, a little adventurous.

. . . Women and men of the Yale College Class of 2002, since you only became Yale students 15 minutes ago, I have the honor to be your first Yale instructor. And behold! After only 15 minutes, you have advanced this far in wisdom. You have learned that anxiety is excitement traveling under a false name, and that the right use of anxiety is not to relieve it but to rechannel it: to use it to fuel the embrace of challenges, not the flight from them. Now that you've learned the right way to worry, I have no further worries on your behalf. I see you here this day on the brink of a great new chapter of your education, which is to say, your life. I know that you will let no part of this opportunity escape you. On behalf of Yale College, I salute you and I cheer you on.

This all sounds great in theory, but how does it play out in practice? This is the subject of this book. Let's get started.

Chapter 1 –
Admission to Yale

Every year, 30,000 students apply for admission to the 1,300 places in an undergraduate class of Yale College. By what alchemy does the Admissions Office at Yale decide which students will fill those 1,300 places?

The answer lies in part in a self-selection process on the part of applicants. The Admissions Office has stated that less than 1 percent of the applicants (about 200 in number) are shoo-ins, another 15 percent (or 5,000 applicants) are highly competitive for admission. That leaves 25,000 applicants, the majority of whom (say 13,000 or 45 percent of applicants) are perfectly well qualified and the balance, or approximately 12,000 applicants are not qualified and should not have applied. Accordingly, 60 percent of applicants (18,000 in number) are qualified and it is an art to choose those who would be accepted–the art of constructing a balanced class of individuals who would reflect diverse backgrounds and skills and who would be able to learn from each other. In making those choices, Yale can only offer admission to about 2,000 (or about 7 percent) of the 30,000 applicants.

I applied to Yale in a different era. In 1964, only 5,500 students applied to Yale, and there was a self-selection process, with the result that only 10 percent of the applicants were not qualified.

1,600 of these applicants (or a whopping 30 percent) were offered admission.

In addition to Yale, I applied to Stanford and the University of Michigan. By then, my older brother had been at Stanford for a year, and I knew that I did not want to be following in his footsteps once again. So, I effectively applied to two colleges. The computer and the Common Application form has made application to ten or fifteen colleges the norm, applications made often on the basis of name recognition only, not a thorough understanding of the fit between a college and its applicants.

In the summer after my junior year in high school, I took a driving trip with my parents to visit colleges in New England. My interviews on that trip revealed to me the caricatures of the various colleges I visited. I came away from my interview at Harvard with the impression that Harvard was academically snooty. I came away from my interview at Princeton with the impression that Princeton was socially snooty. Another informed Yale writer would refer to the former as "the eggheads to the north" and the latter as "the fashion plates to the south". See Chapter 8.

After my interview at Yale, I was convinced it was where I wanted to go. R. Inslee ("Inky") Clark, Jr., then Associate Director of Admissions at Yale, convinced me that the residential college system was exactly what I was looking for. I knew, even at age 18, that I did not want a college where fraternities ruled the social roost. I entered the admissions process for Yale full of enthusiasm.

I was later to discover that alumni play a role in the admissions process. Historically, 80 percent of the students applying to Yale receive a one-on-one interview lasting about an hour with an alum, who then writes a one-page report to the admissions office. After graduation, I became one of these alums. Inevitably, the subject of how to pay for a Yale education comes up in these interviews.

It always surprises applicants, and their parents, to find that there is a national standard or formula for calculating the contribution expected of parents toward the price of a college education and, where that calculation showed a shortfall for the year, Yale makes up the difference from its endowment in the form of loans, scholarships and term time jobs, such as bussing dishes or working in a library. If there is a good fit between Yale and student, there is a way to make it work financially. This is the essence of *need blind admissions* where a student is evaluated for admission on the basis of academic performance and leadership potential without regard to ability to pay.

Periodically, the Admissions Office has conducted training seminars for interviewers in which they would review entire admissions portfolios derived from actual applications. This was very useful since I never had an opportunity to review my own admissions portfolio, including letters of recommendation from my teachers. To permit such review, of course, would have a chilling effect on the candor of teachers writing letters of recommendation.

It was amazing to watch the mind of the admissions officer work. They could tell from the language used in a letter of recommendation whether the author knew the student well or not. They looked for consistency in commentary among all letter writers and discounted letters that were inconsistent with the others.

The admissions officers also drew conclusions from data in the portfolio. For example, one student took the SATs three times, each time scoring nothing but perfect 800s. "What is this kid trying to prove?" was the comment from the admissions officer. The student was rejected. Yale does not want all valedictorians or all perfect test scorers. They want a mix of people.

Furthermore, Admissions Office staff advised us that, if we found a student who really wanted to go to Yale, the student should tell the Admissions Office in some way, shape or form. This advice reflects the *deal making* aspect of college admissions. Finding the right fit between applicant and University is important and applicants need to take some initiative to demonstrate the fit as they see it.

Once admitted, a student finds himself in what has been called *a beehive of activity*. A former Dean of Yale College spent a number of years at the Hoover Institute at Stanford. When asked to describe the difference between a Yale education and a Stanford education, he replied that it is a matter of intensity. Yale is a more intense learning environment. It is a healthy intensity, but it is more intense.

I have described this difference in intensity with the following scenario. If you're seen at Stanford to be working hard, you are shunned, thought of as a nerd. If you are seen at Yale to be working hard, somebody comes over and says, "Hey, what are you doing?" This is a caricature, and perhaps a bit of an overstatement, but more or less true.

With all this as background, I might well ask the question, "How in the world, then, did *I* get to go to Yale?"

Chapter 2 – Preparation

Dink Stover, freshman, chose his seat in the afternoon express that would soon be rushing him to New Haven and his first glimpse of Yale University. He leisurely divested himself of his trim overcoat, folding it in exact creases and laying it gingerly across the back of his seat; stowed his traveling-bag; smoothed his hair with a masked movement of his gloved hand; pulled down a buckskin vest, opening the lower button; removed his gloves and folded them in his breast pocket, while with the same gesture a careful forefinger, unperceived, assured itself that his lilac silk necktie was in contact with the high collar whose points, painfully but in perfect style, attacked his chin. Then, settling, not flopping, down, he completed his preparations for the journey by raising the sharp crease of the trousers one inch over each knee—a legendary precaution which in youth is believed to prevent vulgar bagging. Each movement was executed without haste or embarrassment, but leisurely, with the deliberate savoir-faire of the complete man of the world he had become at the terrific age of eighteen.

Behind was the known and the accomplished; ahead the coming of man's estate and man's freedom. He was his own master at last, free to go and to come, free to venture and to experience, free to know that strange,

**guarded mystery–life–and free, knowing it, to choose
from among its many ways.**

-**Stover at Yale, 1912**

In June of 1964, I was graduated from a large mid-western suburban public high school as valedictorian. I had taken judicious advantage of an evolving advanced placement grading system that awarded five points for an "A" in an AP class, making it possible to earn an average greater than 4.0 on a scale of 1 to 4. Not uncommon in the world but it made me feel special, nonetheless. I even had a letter from President Johnson congratulating me on my accomplishment. Even if I were one of thousands of such recipients, it made me feel special. Furthermore, I had been President of the Student Council, past Class President, semifinalist in the Michigan Mathematics Prize Competition.

I was also a sprinter on the track team–a journeyman sprinter, to be sure, but I was the best we had.

I used to love running on the curve in track spikes--the grip on the ground, the sudden burst of energy, the graceful feel of leaning into the curve and the final bounding to a stop after the finish line, arms swinging rhythmically to maintain balance during the slowdown. I'll never forget anchoring the mile relay team at the Eastern Michigan Relays. It was a regional meet, with all the color and pageantry of flags and banners, run on an indoor eighth-mile track, which meant that races were run on a continuous curve. I took the baton a few paces behind my competitor, but I ran the best race I can remember, overtook my competitor and beat him. As a team, we didn't win anything, not even ranking in the regional meet, but I was on top of the world.

The author, left, on the Berkley High School track team

PRINCIPAL
LOREN S. OVERTON

ASSISTANT PRINCIPALS
FRED BOLENBAUGH
H. LUCILE MORRISON

COUNSELORS
RUTH BARTON
JOSEPH WINE
THOMAS FLETCHER
WILLIAM R. RICHER
MARIE TOWNER
MARGUERITE ZUBER

Dear

The Berkley High School Student Council is proud to inform you that its former president, Kirk Casselman of 10034 Ludlow, Huntington Woods, Michigan, graduated this past June with the highest average ever achieved at our school.

Kirk's average was 4.5 points, the equivalent of an A+, due to the Advanced Placement courses he took. While maintaining this high scholastic average he found time to participate and win athletic letters in cross country and track, was elected an officer of his Sophomore Class, was selected by the faculty as a member of the National Honor Society while a Junior, was elected as a representative to the Student Council and was the Student Council president while a Senior. He was also an active member of the Ski Club, the Choir, and the Varsity Club.

Berkley High School, and especially the Student Council, is sorry to lose Kirk, but we know that whether at Yale University, where he is now enrolled, or in his chosen career, he will always be the great person he has been and will continue to be an asset to his school, his community, his state, and his country.

Kirk is a credit, not only to his parents, but to the millions of teenagers who wish to prove that they are not delinquents but valuable citizens. Many strive to achieve such a record, but not all can attain it.

Respectfully,

Daniel Raleigh

Daniel Raleigh, President

R. Paul Griffith

R. Paul Griffith, Faculty Advisor

RPG:if

THE WHITE HOUSE
WASHINGTON

October 5, 1964

Dear Daniel:

This is to thank you and Mr. R. Paul Griffith
for your letter to the President concerning
Mr. Kirk Casselman. All that you say has
been noted with interest and appreciation and
the President asks if you will be good enough
to pass along to Mr. Casselman the enclosed
photograph. It comes to him with the President's best wishes for a most successful year
at Yale University.

Sincerely,

Ralph A. Dungan
Special Assistant
to the President

Daniel Raleigh
President
Berkley High School Student Council
Berkley High School
2325 Catalpa
Berkley, Michigan

Enclosure

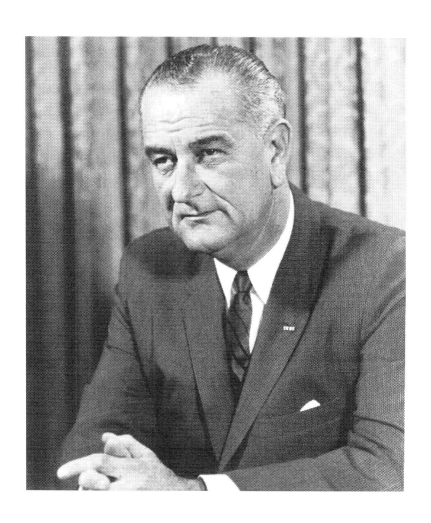

And I was dating the most desirable girl in the high school.

She was Secretary of my Student Council and in my AP classes. I had first laid eyes on her in the ninth grade, when I, as an interloper, attended a dance at the other junior high school that fed into our common high school. There she was across the gym, shadowed by a spotlight in a very high ceiling which bathed her in voluptuous half-light and shadow, a kind of smoky haze. The same image appeared on the cover of the Vassar Night Owls record album a couple of years later when she sang with that group.

A number of benefits accrued to me as result of dating this girl, who shall be known as "my girlfriend" for purposes of this book, not the least of which was that she arranged for me to be taken into the a cappella choir of the high school. Me, with a stone ear and wooden voice and little musical training (I had had one year of accordion lessons before I was 10 years old) singing in a choir!! It was tantamount to a political appointment to the choir.

Being in the choir was one of the most meaningful experiences of my life.

Music has always been important to me, despite my disabilities. My love affair with music started in my extreme youth, listening to late-night radio. Country-western music, liberated in Memphis and other southern cities from competition for the airwaves, would lull me to sleep through the medium of a plastic Motorola combined record player and radio. My first record purchase, a 78-RPM disk for sale at the local Woolworth's dime store, was Chuck Berry's *Maybelline*. My second purchase, now a more modern 45-RPM disk, was *Hound Dog* by Elvis Presley. From there, my collection has grown steadily.

It was in choir that I discovered that there are as many endorphins, nature's pleasure drug, released in the brain from singing as are released from any other activity in which we as human beings indulge. The sheer physicality of singing has as great appeal as yoga or stretching. This sense of well being that accompanies the act of singing is palpable.

And we seem to remember melodies and lyrics more readily than we do poetry or narrative. Music goes to the very soul. Years later, in a white steepled church across the street from a New England country inn, with three inches of snow falling gently, I would remember long passages of the baritone part of Handel's *Messiah.* In the years between these events, however, I would be haunted by a cappella singing at Yale.

My girlfriend played the guitar in a group of girls who sang at high school events, including our English class. She would sing, looking straight at me:

> **I will love you 'til the day I die**
> **I will love you and I'll tell you why**
> **Cause your heart is pure and your dreams are mine**
> **Cause I love you**

I fell heir to that guitar when she upgraded it and I still have it—47 years later.

We spent the summer, my girlfriend and I, doing what kids in the Midwest do in summer, dabbling at summer jobs, working on my car, worrying about proper wardrobe for college, sewing name tags into the proper wardrobe, going to drive-in movies (and all that that entails) and going to the lake. She had been accepted at Vassar, historically the sister school of Yale. No fool I, I wasn't going to an all-male college without my high school girlfriend. We were playing out our futures strictly as planned.

As the summer drew to a close, I got my first exposure to the "Yale community": All of the parents (read "mothers") of local high school students matriculating at Yale got together and conspired for all of us, a dozen or so other members of the Yale Class of 1968, to ride a Greyhound bus together to New Haven.

Well, this turned out to be a false community or, at best, a short-lived community, one that had no real affinity amongst its members. However, the bus trip did provide an opportunity for my girlfriend and me to test our newfound independence and our devotion to each other. The bus made a penultimate stop in New York City, where my girlfriend had arranged a rendezvous, convincing her father to divert their trip to Poughkeepsie in order to surprise me during the layover at the Port Authority Bus Terminal.

And surprised I was! The bus trip had been uneventful, boring at best, and shot through with anxiety over the unknown future. Furthermore, it was probably the longest period of time my girlfriend and I had been apart in many months. Seeking a little privacy, we found a public telephone booth (remember telephone booths?) just big enough to accommodate me with my girlfriend on my lap, with our feet sticking out holding the folding door open, where we proceeded to make up for lost time.

I have no other recollection of that bus trip to Yale. Surprising how selective memory can be.

Chapter 3 – Arriving for the First Time

He passed on through the portals of Phelps (Gate),
hearing above his head for the first time the echoes of
his own footsteps against the resounding vault.

He was on the campus, the Brick Row at his left; in the
distance the crowded line of the fence, the fence where
he later should sit in joyful conclave.

"And this is it–this is Yale," he said reverently, with a
little tightening of the breath.

-Stover at Yale, 1912

The Residential College System

The bus pulled into New Haven and stopped at Phelps Gate, the elaborately carved entryway into the Old Campus. Disembarking from the bus, I could for the first time "hear above my head the echoes of my own footsteps against the resounding vault," a sound I was to hear many times before my time at Yale was over.

The sound took on different meanings at different times. I have to say that the echoing footsteps first evoked an image of a cold and inhumane institutional environment, such as one might find at the entrance to a prison. However, that impression gave way to a more comforting feeling when I realized that passing through the Phelps Gate provided a buffer between the hubbub of the City and the relative serenity of the Old Campus, with its welcoming, twinkling lights at night. Later, it signaled my arrival home, for the Old Campus was home and the echoing footsteps meant I would soon reach my room, my refuge from the rigors of the day. If it were raining or snowing, Phelps Gate provided relief from the weather, if only momentarily.

The Old Campus is a series of buildings of mixed architectural style, built over a period of years but now forming a continuous façade enclosing a green space the size of an entire city block. All freshmen live in dorms on the Old Campus, but "dorms" is the wrong word to describe the suites of rooms that cluster on each of four or five levels or landings accessible via a single entryway door.

This design enhances the creation of community in subtle but distinct ways. A student opening the entryway door is confronted by a set of stairs leading up to a landing. Three or four suites of rooms radiate off the landing, housing four students per suite. So, typically, twelve or more students are housed in a way that they cross paths continually. Multiply those numbers by three or four or five, depending on the number of floors in the entryway, and you have a good sized community of people passing each other many times during the day.

A suite of rooms consists of a large living room or common room and two small bedrooms off the living room. This gives the four students occupying the suite enough room to spread out, but usually not enough room to escape horseplay for study. Students during their serious study time can be found in any one of a number of nooks and crannies in the buildings on campus. The dorm rooms, therefore, become the place to hang out with friends and socialize. This use of space follows naturally if you subscribe to the precept that environment shapes behavior.

This same design of the architecture applies to the twelve

residential colleges, to which a Yale class moves after spending freshman year living all together on the Old Campus, presumably building class cohesiveness. A freshman class of approximately 1,300 students is chopped up into twelve arbitrary groups, each group assigned, before its members ever arrive on campus, to one of the twelve residential colleges.

What is critical is the word "arbitrary". While some effort is made freshman year to put compatible roommates together, the selection of students to populate each of the twelve groups is purely arbitrary. This forces students of widely diverse backgrounds to live together, eat together, study together and even play together. There is no jock house, nerd house, intellectual house or social climber house. Instead, there are elements of all of these in each of the residential colleges.

It was not always so. As late as the 1950s, the housing situation was dramatically different. After living together for one year on the Old Campus, students were free to collect themselves into rooming groups and to apply as a group to whichever residential college they felt comfortable in joining. As a result, each of the residential colleges did take on a distinct personality. For example, Silliman College became the favorite of engineering students at Yale; Branford became the home for jocks, and so on. The housing change in the 1960s underscores Yale's explicit intention to avoid the *flocking phenomenon* and to mix people in the residential colleges.

As a result of the current housing arrangements, I was meeting classmates in my own residential college with whom, for one reason or another, I had not spent time until senior year. The flocking phenomenon, the basis for fraternity and sorority life, is very difficult to defeat. Usually, those classmates I met senior year were very different from me but, having established myself over three years, I felt I could stretch to greet these lately acknowledged classmates. And, usually, they turned out to be pretty interesting people.

The world at large tends to think of Yale as an elitist institution, and, in many respects, it is. However, seen in this context, I think it's fair to say that Yale is a great democratizing institution. The place where this democratizing aspect was first made manifest was in the dining hall. Freshman year the entire class ate together in Commons, a huge dining hall with 40-foot high, wood beamed ceilings. This was the first opportunity for the entire class to mix with each other on a regular basis. (We had to wear coat and tie to meals and may have been the last class facing such a requirement.)

Still, the experience of taking meals at Commons was not an intimate one; the place was too big. It didn't lend itself to communication. The marble floors and high ceilings tended to make it very noisy and, if anything, inhibited conversation and encouraged moving along to get the next thing done.

That was not the case, however, once a student moved into the residential college in sophomore year. There, the class had been divided into twelve groups of about 100 to 125 students each, or 350 sophomores, juniors and seniors altogether, making a much more congenial setting. Lingering over a meal was the watchword, even at breakfast (unless you had a class you wanted to get to on time). The slower pace increased the opportunity for chance encounters. As a result, information was exchanged more readily, friends were made and the building of community progressed.

The residential college was also the focal point for a variety of activities and sports. Photography studios, workshops, exercise facilities, dramatic productions, choruses–even printing presses–were available for students without enough to do otherwise. Intramural athletics, fully outfitted with uniforms and gear and pitting one residential college against another, were available for those without the time, talent or desire for varsity level competition. All this served to inculcate a sense of loyalty to one's residential college. When one Yale graduate meets another, an introduction is almost always followed by the question, "What college were you in?"

My Diverse Classmates

My own freshman year roommates and floor mates illustrate the diversity of the Yale student body. I had three roommates, one from Lake Oswego, Oregon, one from Teaneck, New Jersey and one from the Bronx, New York. Besides the diversity of their origin, these three roommates exhibited vastly different profiles.

Two things struck me about the roommate from Oregon: he was short and he had a crop of red hair. What gave him stature was his sense of humor. Droll and ironic, he would not use humor to cut his listener down to size, but rather to drag himself up by his bootstraps to his listener's height. Secure in himself, he would spend Friday nights listening to music and playing the recorder. A sympathetic character, he was an ideal roommate. He earned a graduate degree in philosophy, then an MBA and eventually became an oil company executive.

My second roommate was a Black American from Teaneck, New Jersey, who played inter-college football, basketball (captain) and track and varsity track, was president of the black fraternity and co-founder of the Black Student Alliance at Yale. A political science major, he was reported to have single-handedly quelled violence in the Hill District of New Haven during the Bobby Seale trial. After earning an MBA from the Yale School of Organization and Management, he worked for a major international consulting firm before starting his own consulting firm.

The third roommate was a taciturn Jewish guy from the Bronx, New York. Awkward in gait and conversation, he seemed destined to become a research doctor. He had limited extracurricular activities but scored high in academics all four years. He is, in fact, an academic medical doctor specializing in cancer research.

We four constituted the denizens of 65 Vanderbilt Hall. But there were others on the floor inhabiting the three other suites of rooms radiating off the landing.

One was the stringer for the *New York Times* from freshman year on. He would spend enormous amounts of time tapping out stories on a typewriter for the newspaper. After a distinguished career as a journalist in various undergraduate publications, he became a lifetime employee of the *New York Times*, including a stint as White House correspondent.

Another was an economics major from the Midwest, who appeared totally focused on his career, apparently not willing to take academic risk in exploration. He went on to lifetime employment with a major bank, of which he became President and Chairman.

A third was known for getting through Yale with the lightest class load and least amount of work possible. His signature activity, mostly indulged in the evening hours, was staring into his tank of tropical fish. Yet, he earned a law degree and became a practicing lawyer.

Another was so compulsively concerned with the weather that he maintained notebooks daily of weather at various sites he was concerned about. Quick to laugh, he became a psychiatrist.

But the award for Most Creative Use of a Tradition went to yet another floor mate whose job it was to write the halftime shows for the Yale University Precision Marching Band (anything but) at the football games. There was a time, in the late 1960s, when discussions were undertaken concerning the merger of Yale and Vassar. To celebrate the impending consummation of this relationship, this floor mate arranged to have half of the Band form a "Y" on the field and half of the Band form a "V" on the field right below the "Y". You guessed it! He arranged for the "Y" to march down directly into the "V" and the big white bass drum at the base of the "Y" to then spin off crazily. This floor mate dropped out of Harvard Law School after one semester to join a Madison Avenue advertising firm.

It would be interesting to determine the extent to which this diverse group of classmates pursued professional careers predictable based their undergraduate careers. Did their Yale experience lead them onto a dramatically new path?

I believe the answer is no, and I base this answer on very

little hard evidence. However, I would turn to the essays written for the hardbound book prepared for our Twenty-fifth Reunion, which contain commentary on professional stature and personal contentment. See my own essay in Chapter 26 but I offer two other examples that follow. While the material in these essays is long outdated, it is twenty-five years in seasoning and does have some credibility for that.

The classmate who was stringer for the *New York Times* was still working for that newspaper after twenty-five years. He had taken assignments in Washington, New Delhi and Tokyo. The assignment in India took him and his wife to the "outer reaches of reality. But we learned that India, with its colossal problems, its spirituality and its intensity, is humanity's center." He served as Chief White House correspondent and rode around the world on Air Force One. In spite of his very interesting career, he wrote, "I have also learned that the greatest rewards come from being a husband and father."

The psychiatrist who was quick to laugh was just as funny twenty-five years after graduation as he was as an undergraduate. He began and ended his Twenty-fifth Reunion essay this way:

With the July 15 deadline looming – do they ever do otherwise? – I am determined *not* to be left out of our Class Book. Yet, I have found it nigh impossible to find a proper voice, let alone a cogent message. My first efforts were punctuated with cries of, "Uncle Alan, when can we go swimming?" and, "Daddy, I want to show you the best picture I've ever drawn in my entire life!"

Nevertheless, let me start by saying that my greatest source of happiness has been my marriage of seventeen years to Susan, who proved a woman could be both "true and fair", and our two daughters, Lilana and Michelle.

. . .

Taking myself so seriously for so many hours has made this a very long day for me and my family. If I stop now, you'll miss out on my lecture on malignant narcissism, entitled "America is Fast Becoming a Third World Country," but then again most of my patients have heard it and will gladly furnish you a copy for a small fee. The question I'm most often asked is, "How in the heck do you listen to all that stuff all day long without getting depressed yourself?" My reply, to paraphrase Mark Twain: "With a little practice, Man can learn to endure any sort of adversity, provided it's not his own." On that note, allow me to subside, mercifully, and give the next "poor unfortunate soul" *his* "15 minutes of greatness. (sic- fame)" I imagine us fading away to strains of Faure's Pavane – at the piano I'll be accompanying Susan on the flute, Lilana on the violin, and Michelle will be singing.

I probably made as dramatic a shift as anyone, from math and economics to art history, but fell back onto my path by going to law school and joining a major law firm. What interests me is the extent to which my diverse classmates rely on their families as the greatest source of satisfaction, not their careers.

The subject of private school versus public school preparation for Yale always comes up in discussions like this. To the extent one can generalize about this topic, I would say there was very little distinction drawn between private school students and public school students once all arrived at Yale. All students realized the honor bestowed on all students accepted to Yale. Oh, there was undoubtedly a chumminess among members of some of the fraternities favoring other prep school students in inviting new pledges, but it was subtle.

The main difference between private and public school students was one of style–of dress and demeanor. You never saw such scruffy Bass Weejuns as were on the feet of many prep school students.

Sleeves of Oxford cloth, button-down shirts were rolled up past the elbow in a haphazard manner. Even their tweed sports jackets had a wonderfully casual, slept-in look. There was a laissez-faire attitude that accompanied this sartorial splendor, which I would come to know as *shabby gentility* when I moved to Philadelphia. If family money and stature didn't prevent problems, they would surely solve them.

Academically, there was no real distinction between prep school students and public school students. Both performed well in some circumstances and both performed poorly in some circumstances. Some of my best friends were prep school students. Others of my best friends were public school students. It didn't matter.

Had it been ten years earlier, or maybe even five years earlier, I might have felt differently about being a public school graduate, but public school winds had been blowing through the halls of Yale since at least the early 1960s. Based on, among other things, the welcome I received during my interview in New Haven, I felt Yale was as much mine as it was theirs.

I would draw a distinction between my coming onto a campus that had historically been dedicated to serving New England prep schools and the advent of women as undergraduates coming onto a campus that had historically been all male. Here, I rely on the experience and opinions of Louise who came to Yale as a graduate student in 1967, several years before the advent of women undergraduates. She experienced borderline hostility in undergraduate classes as a graduate student. Undergraduates would not speak to her, since eligible women were not expected to be on campus during the week. They were a weekend thing. This came as a shock to Louise, since the male to female ratio at Stanford, where she spent her undergraduate years, was 5:3, with highly favorable effect on all women on the Stanford campus. It took a number of years, with increasing numbers of women accepted at Yale, before women were comfortably integrated at Yale.

Applicants and prospective applicants: Never again in your life will you be surrounded by, and have access to, as many broadly talented, competent, interesting and interested people as you will at Yale.

The City of New Haven

One of the first decisions a student in high school must make in applying to college is whether he or she wants a city setting or a suburban or country setting. Yale is set in a city–the City of New Haven, Connecticut. Like many New England towns and cities, it is old. And like many New England towns and cities, it is small, making it possible in a fifteen-minute bike ride to be in rolling Connecticut countryside.

The central part of the city, the heart of the city, was laid out hundreds of years ago on a grid pattern, most of which is dominated by Yale University. Its splendid architecture and grassy courtyards were built in the 1920s and 1930s and completely remodeled and modernized in the last ten to fifteen years. Because of this dominance, the city intrudes on the campus to a very limited extent. There are many venues where one can sit outside and enjoy the sunshine or sniff the air, or set up a volleyball net for a pickup game. In this respect, Yale offers the best of both a city setting and a suburban setting.

Equally important, New Haven has been gentrified. During my undergraduate years in the late 1960s, there were very few upscale stores or restaurants. Now they abound. The Saks Fifth Avenue store is long gone, replaced by the music Mecca Toad's Place, where the Rolling Stones kicked off a world tour some years ago with a surprise concert. Right next to Toad's Place is another music Mecca, Mory's, a private club for undergraduates and alumni that is both tavern and restaurant. Mory's is also home of the famed Whiffenpoofs, the seniors-only a cappella singing group that holds forth every Monday night during the school year.

New Haven was much maligned in decades past and, I must

say, in my era it's reputation was probably deserved. I remember poorly stocked stores and rundown housing especially on the route into the campus by car, leaving the visitor with an unimpressive first impression and an unimpressive last impression. Furthermore, relations between the students and the townies were not good and the threat of violence between the two groups was ever present.

New Haven began to deteriorate in the1950s when its manufacturing base began to move out, downsize or go out of business. Winchester Repeating Arms Company, which produced guns and rifles in New Haven for 140 years, is probably the best-known example of a failed New Haven company. It's fine, handcrafted products required expensive craftsmanship and the company began to become unprofitable by the 1960s, struggled for years with rising costs and went out of business in 2006.

Much of the credit for the improvement in New Haven over the last fifteen or twenty years goes to President Rick Levin (also Class of 1968, albeit Stanford '68) for the development of a partnership with the city and improved town-gown relationships. The University has enjoyed the selfless support of its alumni and, with its multibillion-dollar endowment, was able to buy up a number of commercial properties in the main shopping area. It then installed as tenants the upscale shops New Haven had historically been lacking. In addition, the extensive refurbishment of university buildings and the construction of new buildings throughout the campus have lent a fresh face to the entire university.

Of great importance was Yale's decision to make voluntary payments to the City of New Haven in lieu of taxes. The University contributes voluntary payments to New Haven in part because, as a non-profit organization, Yale does not pay property taxes on much of its land. The voluntary payments and the state-funded Payment in Lieu of Taxes (PILOT) program help reimburse the city for potential tax revenue lost from the Yale-owned property used in a nonprofit capacity. The University wants to continue to be a good citizen in New Haven by helping to keep New Haven strong.

This change took place in the environment of Yale's physical dominance of the City of New Haven. The University reported in the spring of 1995 as follows:

Yale is the largest employer in New Haven. Total employment has grown from 6,000 in 1970 to 9,428 in 1992 and, due to inflation, Yale's payroll has increased over the same period from $56 million to $338 million. Yale's employment represents over 14 percent of New Haven's total employment. And importantly, 35 percent of Yale employees live in New Haven and an additional 36 percent live in the eight towns surrounding New Haven. Even though Yale is exempt generally from New Haven real estate taxes, it still is New Haven's tenth biggest taxpayer and the state government reimburses New Haven for approximately 75 percent of the assessed value of Yale's property.

Discussion then focused on Yale's recent efforts to stimulate economic stability and growth in New Haven. Specific initiatives were discussed, such as the Ninth Square Project, the Broadway renovation, reopening of the Park Plaza Hotel and Mall, and Yale's housing program.

Concerning the housing initiative, Yale will make up to $2,000 per year available for up to ten years for each employee who purchases a house in New Haven. Over 115 employees have taken advantage of the program during its first year. Intentionally, the program has not been targeted to any particular sections of the city and, as a result, the distribution of houses acquired on the program have been widely dispersed throughout the city. Also, employees from all economic segments of the University have participated, from administrators and faculty to union workers.

In particular, the Ninth Square Project of the City of New Haven deserves mention here. Its website describes the project as making downtown New Haven an affordable and exciting neighborhood.

The name "Ninth Square" was given to one of the original nine squares of New Haven's town plot, which was laid out in 1638. It was the last of the city's original squares to be redeveloped, and, as a result, many of its historic buildings were vacant or underutilized. In the early 1980s, the City of New Haven began the process of nominating the area to the National Register of Historic Places. The city's goal was to facilitate private investment in the Ninth Square's historically significant architecture. At the same time, a group of outside investors, planners and preservationists approached the city with an ambitious plan for redevelopment.

Inspired by the energy of the outside group, city staff and citizens came together to plan a revitalized safe, attractive, well-managed, urban district where a diversity of people live, work, shop and play . . . (This development, known as the Ninth Square Project, was completed in 1995.)

. . .

Over 500 residents (were to) live within walking distance of all that downtown has to offer, including Yale University. Newly paved streets, new trees, sidewalks, and historic lighting standards create(d) a safe and attractive place. Local merchants hope that the shopping and nightlife will attract students, workers and visitors. Low-income housing tax credits helped finance the development and provided the guarantee that more than half of the apartments would be affordable to such households. If the neighborhood continues to revitalize, the financing restrictions will keep those units affordable for households with modest means.

New Haven is an hour and a quarter train ride from New York City, making it possible to go to New York even for an evening, although it is likely that all the activity on campus will keep the students there. However, daily excursions to New York were enjoyable. Toward the end of second semester, my girlfriend and I took a trip to Greenwich Village and I reported as follows:

There was a great big dried-up fountain in the middle of a park (called) "Washington Square." There was a guy in a beard standing on the edge pleading a cause, which, though I stood there several minutes, I never quite understood. It was immediate and vital, to hear him tell it tho, to be sure. NYU is a block away, so he may be a student of locution. Ringing this little fountain were a lot of little groups of beatniks clustered around guitarists and small ensembles . . . We went down a little further to fabled Bleecker Street and marveled at the "Bitter End Café" where Peter, Paul & Mary and other greats have gotten their starts–well advertised– and looked at the absurd prices without stopping to try the cuisine. We had hotdogs and sauerkraut from a sidewalk vendor instead . . . After lounging around in the park on the grass, we went to Central Park and watched three different painters painting landscapes in the park–things I didn't really expect to see at all. It was all really a lot of fun.

Chapter 4 –
Academics

"Now, you've got to do a certain amount of studying here. Better do it the first year and get in with the faculty."

"Isn't it worth working for–to win out in the end? And, Stover, it's easy enough when you know how. Play the game as others are playing it. It's a big game and it'll follow you all through life. There it is; it's up to you. Keep your head clear and see straight."

. . . Regan, always bent over a book for the last precious moments, coming and going always with the same irresistible steadiness of purpose . . . He would never allow anything to divert him from his main purpose in college–first, to earn his way, and, second, to educate himself. Stover, with others, had urged him to report for practice, knowing, though not proclaiming it, that there lay the way to friendships that, once gained, would make easier his problem.

-Stover at Yale, 1912

Yale places great emphasis on teaching, as opposed to research, requiring that all professors teach undergraduates in Yale College. Yale's commitment to undergraduate education means that, even in introductory courses, it is possible to have a world-renowned scholar as the regular lecturer.

For example, I was able to take introductory art history with the legendary Professor Vincent Scully, whose tenure at Yale spanned many decades. Architect Philip Johnson once described Scully as the world's most influential architectural teacher. He lectured to packed houses, with both undergraduates and graduate students auditing the course without credit just to be in the audience. Scully began lecturing at Yale in 1947 and in 2004 received the National Medal of Arts, the United States' highest honor for artists and arts patrons.

Professor Scully was passionate about art and architecture. Perhaps more importantly, he could impart a sense of passion about art and architecture to his audiences. It is reported that he became so passionate during one lecture that he actually fell off the stage. The image of Professor Scully with a ten-foot pointer pole, slapping and scratching at the screen where his slides were projected in order to drive home a point in his lecture, is an enduring image of Yale undergraduate academic life.

Patrick Pinnell, architect and photographer, and a former student of Scully, said in his book, *Yale University: The Campus Guide,* that the influence of Professor Scully, particularly his *History of Modern Architecture* course, was paramount in his decision to become an architect and that, but for Professor Scully's ability to see and to teach others to see, he would not have been able to write about how buildings relate to each other and to their respective sites.

Professor Arthur Galston provides another example. Professor Galston was a biologist who made his mark in the late 1940s and early 1950s in plant biology and biological warfare. In 1955, he moved to Yale where he remained for the rest of his career, retiring in 1990. During his tenure at Yale, he conducted research for the Department of Defense on Agent Orange, leading to its banning in 1971. He was one of two scientists first to be invited to visit the Republic of China, also in 1971.

Professor Galston taught my introductory biology course

freshman year. The clarity of his thought and ease of articulation made his lectures comprehensible even to a non-scientist such as I. His class is where I first learned that the study of biology is really the study of chemistry, the study of chemistry is really the study of physics, and the study of physics is really the study of mathematics.

Both these professors were at the height of their careers when I entered Yale and, to be sure, each had graduate students to lead their discussion sections. Yet, both attracted huge followings among undergraduates in introductory lecture courses.

At the other end of the spectrum, other courses were offered in a small seminar setting. In fact, a residential college would sometimes offer as a college seminar, held in one of the common rooms of the college, the same course offered as a large lecture, just to provide an alternative for freshmen and sophomores who might otherwise be condemned to large lectures for all introductory courses necessary to meet distribution requirements.

I had placed out of Freshman English after taking the advanced placement exam, so I qualified to take a sophomore level course. The course I took was held in a lounge in the master's house of one of the residential colleges, with its leaded glass windows suffusing the sunlight that played on the overstuffed armchairs. The class consisted of only six or eight students and a full professor, which meant that review of the reading was an intimate discussion, not a lecture. Needless to say, preparation for class took on an urgency that a large lecture did not. Papers we wrote came back with sufficient red marks that we couldn't help but learn something with each assignment. If this were an elite education, I was all for it.

I also took religious studies in a small seminar setting. The course satisfied a philosophy distributional requirement; I tended to shy away from more mainstream philosophy disciplines (where there was no right answer). Distributional requirements were Yale's way of forcing breadth on its students, who, in order to graduate, had to take at least one course in each of seven areas, such as foreign language, science and the social sciences. Yale still requires distribution of course work consisting of both disciplinary area requirements (humanities and the arts, sciences and social sciences) and skills requirements (quantitative reasoning, writing and foreign language proficiency).

The religious studies seminar, *Protestantism, Catholicism and Judaism in the Modern World*, was conducted in an interesting way, which would only have worked in the small seminar setting. Reading assignments were parceled out at the beginning of the semester and each student was responsible for summarizing the reading for the class and the reading of the summary initiated the seminar discussion. When it was my turn to summarize the reading, I stayed up to three o'clock in the morning polishing my summary.

This seminar also introduced me to the writings of the Jewish philosopher Martin Buber, whose book *The I-Thou* became the foundation for my religious beliefs for the rest of my life. Buber's basic tenet described religion as a personal phenomenon, which obviated the necessity for organized religion. I recently confirmed that description with the head of the Slifka Center at Yale. So, what began as an attempt to avoid Kant and Kierkegaard turned into an important philosophical life building block.

How was I to cope with the intensity of this lineup of classes?

The work habits I developed during my high school years stood me in good stead during my first year at Yale. First semester, I was a Ranking Scholar, scoring in the top 10 percent of my class. Second semester, I was on the Dean's List. And I accomplished that while taking what might be considered the toughest course load I had during my undergraduate career–introductory calculus, English literature, French, religious studies and art history–a diverse and demanding set of courses. I thought as little of that accomplishment as I did of my high school grades. I just did it. I did what was asked of me–no more, no less.

The Dean of Morse College, Bob Fischelis, was keeping an eye out for me and I made sure my parents knew about it. I wrote to them that "Tuesday is my makeup exam. When Dean Fischelis reminded me, he congratulated me on my grades and wished me luck. Maybe I did okay on religion after all. I still don't know the grade."

What was surprising to me was that I did it all trying to limit my workweek to five days.

The agreement I made with myself was that I would work diligently during my days on campus and leave time to be with my girlfriend on the weekends. As a practical matter, I always wound up doing something academic while spending time with her, either in Poughkeepsie or in New Haven. I was, after all, a serious student, or, more appropriately, a student who felt some responsibility, rightly or wrongly, toward my parents who were footing all the bills for my elitist education. And they manipulated my sense of guilt without express reference to my grades, but, nonetheless, I knew what they were intending me to feel.

So I kept them abreast of my progress:

Things are really busy these last two weeks, primarily because of an art history paper and test for which I have a ton of reading to do. They aren't due until the middle or end of April, but I've got to do the reading before I can think about writing 15-20 pages on New Haven's 19th-century architecture. I did get a big fat "A" on the math test last week. Whew . . . one more to go, I think. I haven't gotten my religion test back yet, though. It's easy enough to get 80s for me if I just put in enough hours studying, and that doesn't seem bad anymore.

They knew very well what the effect on me was going to be: If I didn't do well, it was because I was spending too much time with "that girl". In December of freshman year, after reading their suggestion that I date other girls, I wrote a scolding letter home in an attempt to justify the balance of work and play I had put in place, proclaiming that "I'm a more conscientious student because of her." And so it went for the entire year.

I spent a good amount of time during the week doing what I was supposed to be doing and enjoying myself on the weekends, even if I took advantage of my girlfriend (who had studied French in high school) to work on vocabulary and writing exercises in French. It was all part of getting the job done. It didn't feel as though I were doing anything extraordinary; and, in fact, I figured I was doing what everybody else was doing. Just as in high school, I was putting in my time and getting the results I wanted. I was really quite content. In late February, I wrote that

> I organize well enough that I'm not too rushed but it's go, go, go every minute all week. There are times though when I get the feeling that I wouldn't want to be anywhere else doing any other thing any other way. I got it after my English exam and it's a good feeling. And when I finish papers . . . This forced organization is really effective, I think, and I'm really happy with it overall.

Studying French was a perfect example of putting in time to get results. Yale had a highly respected French department with a system for teaching French that was extremely effective. Material was first presented in a book written by the Yale French department, with both literal and phonetic spelling of French vocabulary. The same material was presented a second time in the language lab, where the student had an opportunity to listen and to repeat. Finally, class discussion gave a third review and, by then, I had an 80 percent to 90 percent command of the material.

I did manage to have fun, too. In March, I wrote a letter home:

> Well, the (Yale Prom) turned out to be pretty nice. Duke Ellington played on a big 6-foot platform they had built in

Commons and there were colored lights and the Supremes and a steak dinner with wine before at Morse and all. Very exciting. I borrowed a tux from the 4:20 miler guy downstairs I told you about, so the costs were only for ticket, cleaning his tux and the room. I didn't need to rent a car. Don's date couldn't come so I got his room right across the street from the Old Campus. Thanks for getting the paper to me anyway—and my new driver's license. Last night (my girlfriend) and I went to see Joan Baez and Bob Dylan. We got there about an hour early and watched them warm up and play with microphones . . .

Buoyed by my performance freshman year, I branched out and took history of music and music theory sophomore year. This would turn out to be exactly what Yale wanted me to do—branch out, be adventuresome, pursue subjects of study you won't be satisfied with being ignorant about for the rest of your life, regardless of whether or not you have a high probability of success. My wife and I agree that one of the biggest mistakes we made academically in college was not being more "adventuresome", in Brodhead's words, in electing courses based on the renown of the instructor, regardless of our chances for academic success.

I had Yale knocked. Or so I thought.

One chill fall Saturday evening in my sophomore year, I was sitting in the library of Morse College with my girlfriend waiting for the mixer to start at 8:00 PM and tending to one last detail of homework for the week. Dean Fischelis came up to me and said, "You know what? You're working too hard. 80 percent of what you learn here, you'll learn from other people."

Imagine that.

The academic advisor of my residential college, the guy who was supposed to be watching my academic performance most closely, telling me I was working too hard!

And this was coming hot on the heels of my most successful

academic year ever. What was I to do? Let up and be blamed by my parents for not living up to my potential? Stay the course and run contrary to the good Dean? Somewhere in between?

I was not going to be anybody's puppet on a string. But, at the same time, it was nice not to be working quite so hard, so you can be sure I elected that option. As a consequence, my grades fell.

Chapter 5 – Athletics

After three weeks of brilliancy at his natural position (on the football team) of end, buoyed up by the zest of confidence and success, (Stover) was abruptly called to one side . . .

"I'm going to try you at fullback." . . .

He went without spirit, sure of the impossibility of the thing, feeling only the humiliation and failure that all at once flung itself like a storm-cloud across his ambition . . .

From a position where he was familiar with all the craft of the game, Stover suddenly found himself a novice whom a handful of coaches sought desperately to develop by dint of hammering and driving. His name no longer figured in the newspaper accounts as the find of the season, but as Stover the weak spot on the eleven.

-Stover at Yale, 1912

In freshman year, I fell under the spell of Don Tonry.

Don was a gymnast. He competed in the 1960 Olympics and in the 1962 Pan Am Games, which meant he was a world-class competitor on all apparatus—high bar, parallel bars, vault, floor exercise, rings and side-horse. Now he was coach of the men's gymnastics team, not a varsity sport but a club sport, pursued by those who loved the sport.

Don was also one of the best teachers I've ever had. He could look at you, tell you what you were doing right and wrong, and, when you finally did it right, and you knew it was right because it was easy, you realized you'd done what he said. Now, that's a wordy, and inarticulate, way of describing the messy process of learning a new physical skill, but it absolutely describes the process. Don had a magical ability to see and describe the art of gymnastics.

He was patient, good-humored and caring in his treatment of his protégés. And for me it was a good thing, since it took me a year to learn to swing to a handstand in the middle of the parallel bars. He always taught you to miss a trick before you learned to make a trick. For example, you would first learn to kick up against the wall to learn the skill of being upside down, of stacking your vertebrae in delicate balance. A handstand is not a muscle trick. It is a balance trick.

From the wall, you kick up on the end of training bars, which stood six inches off the ground, allowing you to spin out of any attempt to kick up which failed to produce the desired balance upside down. From there, you would proceed to practice swinging to a handstand on the end the parallel bars, always able to spin out as you had done on the low bars. To graduate to the handstand in the middle of the bars, I needed only to deploy the risk reduction move of spinning out and landing to the side of the parallel bars.

I was so enthralled with what I was learning that I went home and built parallel bars in the backyard to continue working over the summer.

What moved me to get involved in gymnastics?

We had a one-semester gym class requirement freshman year, but I didn't want to take the time travel out to Coxe Cage, a twenty-minute bus ride from campus, to participate in track. After the obligatory posture photo and hundred yard swim, I took to the chinning bar like a man possessed. I had never been good at any activity where I had to get my feet over my head, such as diving or tumbling, so I decided to use my semester of gym to try to rectify the situation.

Besides, I had always had good upper body strength as a result of a weight lifting program I undertook in the eighth grade. I was unable to play football in the eighth grade due to a growth anomaly causing a great deal of pain in my knees. The only cure was the passage of time and the development or hardening of the bone structure. At Yale, I sought to utilize my newfound upper body strength in gymnastics.

Gymnastics provided a constant learning experience. Every day in the gym involved learning something new–and overcoming fear. I've never been involved in an activity, including Alpine skiing for forty years, where overcoming fear was more an integral part of everyday life. As preparation for life, participating in gymnastics was among the best things I did at Yale.

It also provided needed balance (no pun intended) to my academic efforts. Besides giving me release from sitting in a chair in the library with vigorous physical activity, I could even sit in the library, close my eyes and ride the rhythms of my routine in the kind of previsualization that became an integral part of sports coaching philosophy in later years. This would give me a relaxing break even while I studied.

There were side benefits to being on the gymnastics team in that every gymnast automatically qualified to be a cheerleader. (A respectable position given that Yale was an all-male institution at the time.) Not only were you in a position to demonstrate your skills in tumbling, skills that would otherwise go unnoticed due to the low profile of the gymnastics team on campus, but you were also entitled to tickets for your dates on the 50 yard line, seated right below Kingman Brewster.

The time I spent in gymnastics was well spent. It set me up to participate in ballet skiing later in my life. I also had the distinct pleasure, at age 45, of climbing back onto parallel bars for a six-week period. At the end of that period, I could do 60 percent of the tricks in my college routine and improved on one. Needless to say, that was supremely satisfying.

To treat the subject of athletics at Yale adequately would require not just another book, but several volumes. Yale does not give athletic scholarships as such but, in its admissions process, is mindful of the needs of its teams. And, depending on which era is under discussion, Yale may have bragging rights even at the national level. Most recently, last winter Yale's hockey team was ranked number one in the country for a period of eight weeks and this year won the NCAA championship. In the late 1960s, the Calvin Hill and Brian Dowling era, Yale was ranked number sixteen in the nation in football. Before that, Yale had been dominant in competitive swimming. Its women's gymnastics teams have exhibited remarkable consistency in winning in Ivy League competition. All these programs have been developed over many years time and inculcated in their participants a love of competition and success in athletics.

At the same time, Yale athletic teams are generally not populated with the kind of athletes who expect to go on to professional sports status. Accordingly, it is possible for an undergraduate to participate in varsity level competition without the kind of ability or commitment required at a large state school. For those not interested in varsity competition, Yale provides highly organized athletic competition at the inter-college level. These are teams fully outfitted, coached and organized to provide satisfaction to Yale athletes who want to hang onto their athletic prowess and yet want to have fun doing it. Finally, there are pickup games in almost all sports conducted on the grassy surfaces that surround many buildings on the Yale campus.

With all these opportunities, it is no surprise that over 90 percent of Yale undergraduates participate in some organized athletic activity.

Yale Daily News article on the 1966 Connecticut AAU Championships; Copyright 2010 Yale Daily News Publishing Company, Inc. All rights reserved. Reprinted with permission.

Chapter 6 – Music and Other Activities

> Every tree seemed plastered with notices of the awakening year, summons to trials for the musical organizations and the glee club, offers to tutor, announcements of coming competitions, calls for candidates to a dozen activities . . .
>
> He had loved, hopelessly, madly, with all the intensity and honesty of which he was capable, a woman–a slightly older woman–who had played with the fragile wings of this boy's illusion and left them wounded . . .
>
> "And another thing: no fooling around with women; that isn't done here . . ."
>
> -Stover at Yale, 1912

You can imagine, based on my high school choir experience, the excitement with which I faced my time at Yale where a cappella singing was an entrenched institution with some fifteen singing groups, each with a dozen or fifteen singers. There were also the Yale Glee Club, the Freshman Glee Club and various residential college choirs. Without much preparation (I was a busy man, after all), I determined to try out for the Freshman Glee Club.

The name Fenno Heath (or, more properly, Fenno Follansbee

Heath, Jr.) has for decades been synonymous with music at Yale. As an undergraduate, he sang with the Freshman Chorus, the Yale Glee Club, the Spizzwinks (?) (Yes, that's how it's spelled.) and the Whiffenpoofs, the prestigious a cappella group for seniors only who have worked their way up the ladder of the other groups, the best of the best. He directed the Yale Glee Club from 1953 to 1992, during which time he was responsible for numerous arrangements of classics, such as *Ave Maria, September Song, Shenandoah, Sometimes I Feel Like Motherless Child, Softly* and *This Train*. Much loved by Yale undergraduates, he was the recipient of many awards for his contributions to the University.

The oldest collegiate a cappella singing group in the country, the Whiffenpoofs were formed in 1909 and were named after the mythical creature in the 1908 opera *Little Nemo* by Victor Herbert playing in New York City. The group called the Spizzwinks (?), the second oldest collegiate a cappella singing group in the country, was formed shortly thereafter, and perhaps in reaction to, the Whiffenpoofs. No doubt, there was an element of one-upsmanship in the apparent attempt to "out-whimsy" the Whiffenpoofs.

It was with understandable nervousness that I approached the oversized double doors of Hendrie Hall, which clanged shut behind me. I was in the clutches of the legendary Fenno Heath. A Whiffenpoof in his day, and by then a Yale icon, he was now my musical executioner. My services would not be needed.

I had been found out. My political clout from high school carried no weight here.

Still, the music was going on around me and it was exciting. Yale had the most highly developed network of singing groups in the Ivy League–and the best. There were impromptu concerts in the dining halls, formal concerts in Woolsey Hall and Dwight Chapel. Music was everywhere, usually with comedic introductions, providing needed, if momentary, calm and good humor to the harried listener. For me, it was one of the nicest aspects of the Yale experience.

But it was also the undoing of my private world.

I have described how I had built my life around, first, studying and, second, being with my high school girlfriend, to the exclusion of other potential friends from among my classmates at Yale and how my residential college Dean advised me that I was working too hard. In my sophomore year, things began to unravel.

My girlfriend, who easily had the talent to qualify for the Vassar Night Owls, went on the singing group circuit and, since Vassar and Yale had long been associated with each other as educational institutions, the groups exchanged concerts on a regular basis. The Yale singing groups had an inherited social cachet that they wore like a mantle and one of them had an eye on my girlfriend.

Other winds were blowing at the same time. My parents did not like me spending all my free time with my high school girlfriend. Their motive was not clear to me, but they made their opinion plain and reinforced it using money, and guilt, as weapons. So when Spring Break rolled around sophomore year, my girlfriend entreated me to join her in West Palm Beach, where the Night Owls were repairing for a series of concerts over the break.

I didn't have the money for such a trip, nor did I expect that a special request for funding from my parents would be met with much success. Accordingly, I answered each entreaty from my girlfriend with the same response. Finally, in frustration, and hoping to end the debate, I snapped, "Oh, go ahead. You won't pine away!"

Little did I know that this comment set the stage for my rival to do more than just eye my girlfriend. I'll never know the details of that Spring Break, although my girlfriend told me much later that the reason she lobbied so hard for me to go to Florida with her was that she knew she was going to be asked out. Whether she knew that and why she didn't tell me that in advance I can't know, but the consequences for me were disastrous.

By College Weekend, she was gone.

College Weekend was the rite of spring celebrated in each residential college in mid-to-late April. It was the last, big weekend of the school year and consisted of picnics on the grass in the college courtyards and events such as the piano smash, wherein an old upright piano was systematically dismembered and passed, bit-by-bit, through a small hoop. I had hoped I would have had a chance to patch things up with her, but my calls to her went largely unanswered.

I took some solace from the fact that, on that particular weekend, I competed in the Connecticut state Amateur Athletic Union gymnastics meet and won a gold medal in parallel bars and a silver medal in vaulting. As I look back at that weekend, I should have taken more comfort in those medals, since in some respects they heralded my own forced independence and the beginning of the realization that I had to rely on myself, and only myself, for my own happiness. Only when that realization finally hit home, many months later, could I hope to share my life and time with the woman who became my wife.

Later, in June, I ventured tentatively to Poughkeepsie where my girlfriend was participating in the graduation exercises at Vassar as a member of the Daisy Chain, a group of sophomore girls who marched in procession, appropriately enough, hanging onto a long, thick chain of daisies, a tradition mired somewhere in ancient Vassar history. While that event was a happy one for most participants, it was clear that my girlfriend was just tolerating my presence. I have rarely felt so lonely. Little did I know the agonies that lay ahead.

Self-doubt, Brewster's second stage, was creeping into my life. Certainly, I was discovering that not all my assumptions about myself and my Yale world were beyond question. In fact, the very foundation of my Yale world was beginning to crumble.

Chapter 7 – Fraternities

"Then there are the junior fraternities; but they're large, and at present don't count much, except you have to make them. Then there are what are called sophomore societies." He hesitated a moment. "They are very important."

"There's a whole mass of us here who are going to fight the sophomore society system tooth and nail, and I'm with them."

"(O)ne dozen of the happiest-looking sophs you ever saw went reeling back to the campus. They were torn and scratched, pummeled, bruised and bleeding, soaked from head to foot, shot to pieces, smeared with paint, not a button left or a necktie--but they were happy!"

"Why happy?"

"They had given Regan the (beer) shampoo."

-Stover at Yale, 1912

I knew at age 18 that I did not want a college where fraternities ruled the social roost. It was the residential college system that immediately caught my eye when I was visiting college campuses.

I knew there were fraternities at Yale, but they were not deemed to be important and, in the fall of my sophomore year, I determined not to rush the fraternities. However, seeing the Yale fraternity system beginning to operate that fall and winter in an acceptable manner, I decided to give it a go in the spring rush. In a letter home, I rationalized it this way:

> The only reason I have for joining a fraternity would be for the chance to meet a lot more people, primarily, and for expanded social opportunities–they have dances every Saturday and mixers arranged about once a month . . . I wasn't enough enthused last Friday to think I'd want to be in one for the next two years, but I think there might be something to it if I only wanted to spend the money for a year. Most seniors aren't really active anyway . . . At best, I'm a little cool to the idea myself but I think there might be some value to it. Tell me what you think . . .

Rushing a fraternity, of course, involved an initiation and an acceptable level of hazing–sitting around on the floor of the fraternity house in underwear being verbally abused and berated by those who had undergone a similar routine the previous fall. During the initiation, one of the initiators made the telling comment that, as Yale undergraduates, we're already part of the biggest fraternity on the East Coast. That comment reinforced the view that the fraternities really were unimportant and, after three months, I quit the fraternity and my Yale experience was not diminished.

There's no doubt in my mind that there is a role for fraternities even at a place like Yale where the whole undergraduate infrastructure has a more democratizing motivation. The flocking phenomenon is too strong to be resisted, particularly by the insecure teenager on his first sojourn away from home. Still, the residential college system obviates the necessity for fraternities to provide the sole measure of social success. As an adjunct to the residential college system, fraternities do provide an extra measure of social security, and one more party on the weekends, for those who need it.

That spring, I bought a BMW R600 motorcycle belonging to an upperclassman who had taken it on the infamous singing group trip to Florida. In a way, I imagined that I had emasculated my rival by denying him access to the tool he used to woo my girlfriend. Whatever my intention, purchasing the motorcycle had no effect on my social life. It did, however, open the door to new adventures and, as such, was a liberating move on my part.

I shipped the motorcycle home in a crate so I could learn to drive it safely over the summer. I rode it daily and got pretty comfortable in the saddle. When I reported a small problem with the front brake to my father, I found him and a neighbor taking the front wheel apart, much to my consternation since it was my life they were tinkering with. I did discover, on the other hand, that my father rode an Indian motorcycle when he was in Washington, D.C. in law school, which I probably never would have discovered under any other circumstance.

All this legitimized my owning the BMW and paved the way for my big adventure, which was to be riding for two full days back to New Haven when school started in the fall.

BMW Photo by Yale Daily News

Chapter 8 –
Senior Societies

"What do you know about the society system here?" said Le Baron abruptly.

"Why, I know–there are three senior societies: Skull and Bones, Keys, Wolf's-Head–but I guess that's all I do know."

. . .

"It has its faults. But it's the best system there is, and it makes Yale what it is today. It makes fellows get out and work . . . The seniors have fifteen in each; they give out their elections at the end of junior year, end of May. That's what we're all working for."

. . .

They went out and passed Vanderbilt toward their eating-joint. Off the campus, directly at the end of their path, a shape more like a monstrous shadow than a building rose up, silent, ivy-covered, blind, with great, prison-like doors, heavily padlocked . . .

"Which is it?" said Stover, in a different tone.

"Skull and Bones, of course," said McCarthy defiantly. "Look at it under your eyelids, quick; don't let anyone see you."

. . .

"To be one of fifteen–only fifteen!"

. . .
"I think there've got to be some reforms made; they ought to be kept more democratic."

"I think we want to keep away a good deal from the social admiration game–be representative of the real things in Yale life . . . we've all got too much of this society idea in our heads; but, since they exist, it's better to do what we can to make them representative and not snobbish."

-Stover at Yale, 1912

While we're on the subject of senior societies, we might as well dispense with that subject even though it interrupts the chronology developed in my narrative. To explain the phenomena of Yale senior societies, I could do no better than to quote at length from an article by Lanny J. Davis '67, '70L, who became lawyer, author, consultant and TV commentator, and who was in his senior year the student Chairman of the *Yale Daily News*, probably the most prestigious office on the campus. The article was published in my Senior Class Book, which chronicles events of our senior year and provides a face-book review of the entire class.

Briefly, the memberships consist of men who have distinguished themselves in some activity at Yale–intellectual, social or athletic. Chosen by the out-going delegation of seniors, the new members meet twice a week–unfailingly– for the following year, accepting the ritual and tradition that has passed through countless delegations . . .

This is what the "ideal" group will consist of: a football captain; a Chairman of the *Yale Daily News*; a conspicuous radical; a Whiffenpoof; a swimming captain; a notorious drunk with a 94 average; a filmmaker; political columnist; religious group leader; a Chairman of the Lit.; a foreigner; a

ladies man with two motorcycles; an ex-serviceman; . . . and
a guy nobody else in the group had heard of, ever.

There are at present eight societies at Yale with *tombs*,
known curiously as the *abovegrounds*. Between eight and
ten more flourish *underground*, ostensibly without granite
trappings . . . Fifteen members belong to each society–with
only a couple of exceptions, bringing the total number of
seniors involved to about 275, or a little over one-fourth of
the class . . .

As the oldest, and traditionally the most prestigious, of the
societies, Skull and Bones has the streamers of 135 years of
rumors clinging to its ugly walls. Secrecy undoubtedly adds
to an institution's mystique, and there is no society that
flaunts its secrecy more self-importantly, or is more prey to
rumor, than Skull and Bones. Thus, more than one junior
has remarked, "Sure, I'll accept Bones if I get a tap. I'm too
damn curious–something amazing must go on."

(Among its alumni,) Bones can quietly point to Henry
Stimson, MacGeorge Bundy, Yale Chaplain William Sloane
Coffin, William F. Buckley, Henry Luce, John Hersey,
Archibald MacLeish, Robert Taft and Alonzo Stagg . . .

In terms of rudimentary purposes and form, all the societies
are patterned after Bones, which was formed in 1832. In
that year, a number of juniors spuriously protested what they
considered an injustice in the elections offered by Phi Beta
Kappa, and rebelled to form their own group. Adopting
a death motif, they carried on about the Yale campus,
bearing skulls and crossed thighbones and parading with
torches . . .

And remember *Stover at Yale*? The All-American college boy

at that All-American college midway between the eggheads to the north and the fashion plates to the south. Champion wrestler, star football player, and a gentlemanly lover, Dink Stover's fabulous career is followed no further than the end of his junior year. For author Owen Johnson bestowed on his hero the supreme accolade: a tap from Bones. There was simply no need to continue the narrative, for any further achievement would have been anti-climactic.

Tap Night is the evening in late May when all the senior societies designate, or tap, the succeeding delegations. Tap Night is preceded by conversation between the seniors of the existing delegation and their putative successors among juniors. From these conversations, juniors derive some insight as to their potential to be tapped by any given society.

You can imagine the tension developed among the juniors who may be expecting to be tapped by one or more of the senior societies that have shown interest during the pre-Tap Night period. There is an appointed hour, say, 8:00 PM, when the senior delegations make their selections known and they do so by positioning a senior delegate outside the room of the junior prospect. For their part, juniors are expected to remain in their rooms until the appointed hour.

He, or she, stands silently, some might say mysteriously, outside the room of the junior prospect. When the bells in Harkness Tower announce the hour, the senior delegate announces the name of his society and asks, "Accept or reject?" The onus then shifts to the junior prospect, now freed from the anticipatory confinement to his room, to accept the tap, foreclosing a potential option with a more coveted society, which could be coming later in the evening, as the last positions are filled.

The air is made thick with the weight of the choice, while one's position in Yale society is determined.

Based on the course I had charted for myself through Yale, I did not rise to the level of an aboveground senior society; however,

I did qualify for an underground. As with the fraternities at Yale, I believe there is a role for the senior societies in the sociology of Yale. The primary focus of the society meetings is the autobiography or personal history. Each member of the society is allocated one evening meeting in which he is expected to give an account of his life, while the rest of the members listen, analyze and offer commentary on the personal history presentation.

The senior society experience is essentially the ultimate distillation of the residential college system. Once again, the flocking phenomenon expresses itself at Yale in an observed traditional diversity. Remember that the societies recognize leadership in a variety of fields–intellectual, athletic and social–in choosing the successor membership. Society membership signals one last chance to get to know a variety of people from among one's classmates on an intimate basis. As such, it has both the elements of elitism and an "individualistic, almost anarchistic, definition of democracy", in Brewster's words.

When freshman first I came to Yale, senior societies were certainly part of the vocabulary, if not part of the conversation, and the aboveground tombs, conspicuous as they were with their windowless vault-like appearance, were a constant reminder, but a reminder of what? The sociology of the place, as caricatured in the previous quotes from *Stover at Yale,* mandated a laissez-faire attitude toward senior societies.

Just as I was pleased to have decided to join a fraternity, I was pleased to have been tapped for an underground senior society. By the fall of my senior year, I was in the final stages of rediscovery and mature ambition and was levelheaded enough to have seen the value of indulging in my diverse classmates for one last time.

Before discussing the activities of my own senior society, I will describe facilities and activities of a generic aboveground. My information derives from a number of sources over the years since graduation. For example, Bob Fischelis, who was the Dean of Morse College and became a lifelong friend, also served as advisor to one of the abovegrounds, attending their meetings and inevitably commenting, either in the course of a meeting or afterward one-on-one, on the affairs of the society members. He invited Louise and me to tour one of the tombs. On another occasion, one of the aboveground societies held an open house and discussed their history.

The typical aboveground tomb has a large dining room and kitchen with a cook who prepares dinner for the fifteen members meeting on Thursday evenings. There is likely to be a rack holding numerous glass bottomed beer steins. Tradition has it that these belonged to former members and, when they die, the glass in the bottom of the stein is broken. There is also a large living room where the biographies are given and rooms where out-of-town guests or former members can be housed overnight. As one might expect, the facilities have had decades of hard use by undergraduates.

The underground societies, like my own, were patterned after the abovegrounds, but, as the name implies, had no permanent structure. We met in a rented house at the edge of campus and our meetings were not as elegantly staged as the abovegrounds. Instead of the dining room, we might have ordered pizza and eaten in the living room.

Whether aboveground or underground, the activity was the same: each member had an evening dedicated to his presenting his life story in whatever manner he chose. Other members of the society would listen intently and offer comment, generally of a sympathetic or helpful tone. It was surprising the number of times members had similar experiences or could help each other with personal problems. Again, remember that, in choosing the next delegation, members of a society sought a diverse group of classmates. Being in a senior society was an exercise in creating community and getting to know people of a different stripe. It was effective preparation for the real world.

However, the senior societies at Yale have always been controversial, which is the reason I lavished so much space to the quotes from *Stover at Yale* at the beginning of this chapter. The battle between social admiration and snobbishness, on the one hand, and democracy and the real things in Yale life, on the other hand, seems to have been perennial throughout Yale's history, and probably always will be.

Chapter 9 –
Junior Year –
On the Way Down

J unior year. It was to be the best year, and the worst year, of my
life at Yale.

It began with my ride from Detroit to New Haven on the BMW.
The trip set the pace for the entire year. Fortunately, the front brake
assembly had been reassembled in a timely fashion, permitting an
on schedule departure for New Haven. Unfortunately, the driveshaft
broke down three hours into Canada. So there I sat, waiting for
my mother to come with a trailer to haul me home in ignominious
retreat.

My spirits were buoyed when a *real* motorcyclist stopped to see if
I needed any help. He had seen my Yale cheerleading sweater draped
over my handlebars (a sign for my mother to stop) and concluded, I
suppose, that I was no Hell's Angel. Since he was alone and dressed
as your everyday motorcyclist, I concluded that he was no Hell's
Angel. I allowed as how my mother would be along shortly and he
smiled and went on his way.

The repair of the driveshaft took only a day or two and I was on my
way again. It was exhilarating to be on a motorcycle covering two full
days of travel. The aches in my body which settled in from too long in

one position, battling the forces of the wind at 70 miles an hour, were relieved by shifting from the front seat to the back seat of the motorcycle and stretching my back. An occasional slalom course in and out of the white, dashed lines on the highway provided amusement.

Hours passed quickly since the novelty of the trip did not wear off readily. Stopping for meals gave me opportunity to swagger up to the lunch counter as cool as you please. I was becoming a motorcyclist.

As night began to fall, I picked a suitable field to sleep in, figuring that in Canada in the1960s I would be safe enough. Besides, the tall grass made me all but invisible and I slept soundly throughout the chilly late summer night.

Awakened by the warming sun, I immediately set out on the last leg of my journey, the exhilaration of the day before motivating an early start. The second day was easily as much fun as the first day. I crossed the border from Canada into New York State and aimed for Poughkeepsie, where I had hoped to find my girlfriend settling in to begin her junior year at Vassar.

The exhilaration of the last two days began to crumble when I pulled onto the Vassar campus, which was largely deserted. I had planned the trip to arrive at Yale a few days early so I could enjoy the Yale campus in a quiet period. I don't know why I expected my girlfriend to be in residence, but, nevertheless, when I tried to reach her in Raymond House, my crumbling exhilaration quickly turned to despair.

Thus began my junior year.

Little did I know that I was leaving Brewster's self-doubt stage and was about to enter the festering stage of self-pity. I was entering an emotional roller coaster ride.

Chapter 10 –
Junior Year – The
Utter Nadir

Things got no better as students filtered back onto the campuses of both Vassar and Yale. My telephone calls to my girlfriend either went unanswered or consisted of quarrelsome conversations leading nowhere. We kept in touch, however, which was probably not a good thing. For example, she loaned me her car to drive to a gymnastics meet at the Merchant Marine Academy one weekend she was visiting in New Haven. While a nice convenience for me for the weekend, the encounter shot one further arrow through my heart and soul.

I began to wake up each morning feeling a crushing weight on my chest, a sign I was later to learn reflected a deepening depression that persisted to varying degrees for the entire school year. I tried to put it into words:

> This is going to be not a very good year. My econ courses are not interesting me yet. You know about the trouble I'm having with (my girlfriend) and this is a bad place to be alone in and it's taking a lot out of me to readjust. Sure I've

got lots of time now but I have no motivation. Maybe it's too much time.

My cycle and gymnastics both make me pretty happy and cheerleading breaks up the weekend, but there is no beauty nor fun nor anticipation nor need nor reason to plan any more. I dress better during the days and that lifts my spirits and helps my attitude, but that's small compensation and certainly no reason to want to work. If I had a burning desire to do what I'm doing, that'd be good–but I have a sneaking disrespect for my proposed major, and that's not good. French intimidates me. I'm putting most of my faith in history of music and drawing.

I guess one thing we both noticed is that when I fall, I fall hard and I live in a world where falls are tough. This is one of the toughest heights I've ever fallen from and right now living from day to day is not easy. I have enough faith in law school that it doesn't contribute to the unrest, but I feel no real drive and the weekends are long and unproductive.

I don't like living this way and the next three months are really going to be important. I can't plan far enough ahead now to know if I want to try to go to Europe next summer and I'm not very excited about giving time to the group which can send me. I'm built funny I guess. Thank goodness for my cycle, gymnastics and cheerleading. When the weather gets bad I won't have one of them.

What it amounts to is this: I don't expect much of me–I'm not very good at this. There's so much to life that I don't have now and that I feel is passing by me, that it's hard to think and memorize and concentrate. I'll be okay just because during the week I work pretty hard, but I don't have that extra oomph I used to have.

My mindset reached its utter nadir one night in the late fall when I got as drunk as I think I have ever been in my life. Itching for a fight, for the only time in my life, I somehow stumbled from Morse College to Calhoun College to the lair of my rival. I cannot remember what I might've said, but the people in the room in which I found myself, whom I assumed to be roommates, knew I was as much a danger to myself as I might have been to anyone else. They calmed me down, or at least diverted me, telling me there was no one there for me to see, and coaxed me on my way.

Outside the College, I hauled myself unsteadily to the top of the wall that surrounded the College. Luckily, the wall had a backrest; otherwise I probably would have pitched backwards into the moat-like abyss that was built around most colleges on the campus. I sat there for some time, my knees pulled up to my face, crying.

Like an apparition in the dark, my girlfriend appeared below me, colored only by the strange glow of the streetlights high above us. I can't remember what either one of us might've said at that time, but I was sufficiently consoled that the rest of the evening passed without incident.

I had entered Brewster's third stage–self-pity. Not only were my assumptions about myself and my Yale world questioned, but all my support systems, the very foundation of my personality and achievements, were gone. Life had become very difficult, indeed.

Chapter 11 –
Junior Year –
Headed Back Up

(H)e had fought down that weakness and learned to look on a soft cheek and challenging eye with the calm, amused control of a man, who invincibly henceforth would cast his life among men. There was not much knowledge of life, if any, that could come to him. He did not proclaim it, but quietly, as a great conviction, heritage of sorrow and smashing disillusionments he knew it was so. He knew it all–he was a man . . . -

-Stover at Yale, 1912

I had to do something.

I started by getting a new group of friends. I followed up by dating some new young ladies. And I changed my academic major. I had come to the conclusion that every individual was responsible for his own happiness. And so I would be.

In February, things began to look brighter but I had to set the record straight for my parents, so I wrote:

I've learned to live without (my girlfriend). I'm just not totally maladjusted like I was last fall. But I'm certainly not as happy as I was the first two years–as happy with myself. That's evidenced by my work. I used to work well and steadily all week long–grind, if you will–but it was very satisfying. I had the work under control, and I felt good working hard. Now I think nothing of just not working at all some night if nothing is pressing. Like, tonight. I'm going to a movie. Then weekends are a race just to do something, and maybe have a bad time. It's so easy to take to just messing around doing foolish, stupid things like a high schooler. This year has been far less rewarding than the first two. I almost feel as though I'm getting less mature.

There were acquaintances in Morse College who became friends. We never discussed my recent history but I suspect they knew what I was going through. They, as much as anything, saved me. Friends became roommates and I added new friends to my list. I began to take pride in the quality of people around me. We indulged in whimsical activities, from the simple to the complex. We played upside down Frisbee–catching and throwing Frisbees while hanging upside down from the branch of a tree in the Morse courtyard. We hosted a black tie art opening by transforming our entryway, complete with draped bunting, into *La Galerie de Grand Manque de Valeur*, featuring such works as a melted and shredded phonograph record of speeches by Everett Dirksen painted white so it looked like Dirksen's hair. Toward the end of March, I wrote home:

> Hey, look for me in the next issue of the alumni magazine, either in a motorcycle pictorial essay or for exploits of yesterday . . . We (were) firing rockets up from the courtyard. One stuck in a tree yesterday and the only one who could scale the tree for ten or twenty feet to handholds was someone with some small gymnastics ability. As I stood up there shaking the tree, an alumni magazine photographer shot several pictures. Watch for them.

Rooming assignments coming up. Will probably be with a whole new group of people next year, who are little more fun than present company. Should be great if it all works out.

Job in Paris is as sure as it can be without knowing all details. I know the new vice president of AIESEC who assured me. But what sacrifice: my cycle, my summer's earnings, and, ultimately, my senior year will suffer. What a decision.

Have a ride to Florida planned with Steve Baker. We'll go to Nassau from there. Will be able to water ski also. Should be great fun. May not bother with the Connecticut AAUs this year.

My first foray into dating other women was local. I picked up a date from Albertus Magnus College on my motorcycle. Hell, the motorcycle thing worked for my rival; why not for me? Well, that wasn't as much fun as it was supposed to be, so I broadened my perspective. I went to a mixer at Vassar. Why not?

There, I danced with a girl who wore a dress with the word "LOVE" emblazoned vertically from the neck to the knee, with the "O" cut out around her navel and the "V" strategically placed. She later told me I was the only one who asked her to dance who did not immediately mention the dress. We agreed to see each other again—and we did. I took quiet pride in that.

And I changed my academic major.

I had started out as a math major, steeped in my arrogant self-confidence and seeking to build on my past strength. Actually, I really enjoyed studying mathematics. There was almost always a single right answer, for one thing. For another, it yielded to effort. Simply put in time and eventually you got the right answer. Memorize a system of theorems and definitions and then solve problems within that system. It was like working a puzzle. The same learning procedure applied to the study of tax law when I got to law school and, according to my son, to software development.

After three semesters of calculus and one of linear algebra, I did a proof on an exam and I knew it was right because the left side equaled the right side, but I had no idea what I'd done. I spent an entire semester memorizing theorems and definitions and applying them to problem sets, but I had no idea what it was used for, why anyone would want to do that–a problem with Yale's theoretical approach to education.

I had begun by then to combine math with economics as a joint major–to bring math into the real world, but economics was known as the dismal science and indeed it was. I said to myself, "I hate this shit. If I only have three semesters left at Yale, I'm going to do something I really love."

So my minor, art history, became my major. Fortunately, I had taken both studio art and art history right from freshman year. I had some discoverable talent in drawing and a facility for mathematics; I thought this meant I would be an architect. I had experimented with this idea until I saw the level of talent and type of temperament exhibited by the guys who really were going to be architects and I didn't fit. Still, I liked the aesthetic aspect of studying art and I liked the eccentricity of those who pursued art.

And Yale let me do it! Even though it meant that I would have to spend three semesters cramming in coursework to complete an art history major in time to graduate. It also meant that I would not be writing a senior thesis, normally a work required by Yale and an academic challenge, to be sure. I think this was the good work of Dean Fischelis of Morse College who must surely have granted me leniency.

It would be just like Bob to do something like that. Bob had been a Harvard undergraduate, a varsity squash player and was now a graduate student in political science. When I was in law school at Columbia, he took me as a guest to the Yale Club in New York, spotted me eight or ten points in squash and kept spotting me additional points until I came close to winning a game. He also sang the deepest bass solo mankind has ever heard in *The Twelve Brigands* with the Yale Russian Chorus. He had an encyclopedic knowledge of the students under his jurisdiction, and even some who weren't, and he kept track of all of them, providing advice and facilitating communication among them.

Years later, sitting in the Harvard Stadium watching the Yale-Harvard football game, I spied Bob Fischelis walking along the sideline with his arm around a student's shoulder and I remarked to my wife, "Bob has a student in tow and all's right with the world."

The decision to change my major set me up for the next milestone in my life–the decision to go to law school. Architecture school was out, as I have said; and business school was in disrepute. (Remember, this era was the height of the Vietnam War and the youth rebellion was in full flower.) I had no interest in graduate school in any academic discipline, so law school was it by default.

In a positive vein, Columbia Law School was selling itself as having just received $6 million from the Ford Foundation to set up combined law and urban studies programs, and it was the history of architecture and regional land-use planning that sparked my interest in the art history department at Yale. So there was a good argument in favor of my going to law school.

This period marked the beginning of Brewster's fourth stage–rediscovery. I had wandered, lost in Brewster's terms, for close to two years. Now, I was in the process of finding myself, a process that would go on for some time. During this period, I formulated three important rules for myself:

1. Every individual is responsible for his or her own happiness.
2. You sometimes lose interest in things for which you have talent; and you sometimes become interested in things for which you have no talent.
3. The whole point of a liberal arts education, and in fact

the whole point of being alive, is to push yourself in as many different directions as you have interest or talent.

With these rules in mind, then, I set about to reconstruct my life. I somehow recovered my sense of humor, regarding the women in my life with a calm, amused control of a man, in Owen Johnson's terms. By far, the most important character trait of this rediscovery period was my sense of humor. I cultivated it and used it as a bridge to other people, men and women, and was delighted to watch it work at creating a community of people around me. I was actually becoming happier than I had been with my girlfriend around, although I had no intention to "invincibly henceforth . . . cast (my) life among men." I missed the feminine touch, the feminine point of view, the verbal sparring that inevitably evolved in my relationships with women. Furthermore, I had always had a girlfriend; I wondered how the guys from all-male prep schools ever got along.

In any event, the stage was set for my next encounter with the feminine mystique.

Chapter 12 –
Summer in France

I had to keep dreaming up exciting things to do. By the middle of my junior year, I had had two and a half years of French language study. Yale also had one of the country's largest chapters of AIESEC, the Association Internationale des Etudiants en Sciences Economiques et Commerciales, essentially a job exchange program for internships in countries all over the world. This was the summer my girlfriend was to be married, so I decided to try to spend the summer after junior year in France.

It was a simple matter, really. I put in an hour or so a week working in an office in New Haven setting up jobs for foreign students in the United States and was rewarded with an internship in a bank, Société Bordelaise du Crédit Industriel et Commercial, in Toulouse. It was to be the first of many trips I would take to France over the coming decades.

It was a nothing job—counting money was the only constructive thing I did, as I recall. The bank employees were very kind to me, showing me the various operations in the bank and taking me to lunch.

The real value of the summer was learning that there are really only 150 words and phrases used daily by the French people and, once you commanded some of those, you could carry on a decent conversation. And the French only really care that you try to use their language. And, if you did try, they were so pleased that they were willing to help you learn.

There were a dozen interns from all over the world in Toulouse that summer, each one struggling to perfect his or her French. The requirement to speak only French was alluded to by our student hosts with *la douche*, having water thrown in your face. The penalty, however, was only good-naturedly referred to, never enforced.

While I was in Toulouse, I made a good friend of François Delouis, who was in charge of the internship program. One night we sat in a café and he paid me a supreme compliment. He drew the following three diagrams on a napkin and I reported his comments in a letter home which follows the diagrams:

Francois' diagrams

(François told me) that he went through periods of being up when he worked unselfishly for AIESEC–all this in French, it's so strange to think about now–and periods when he threw it all off and just couldn't care. (He drew the first diagram above to characterize his mood swings.) He drew a line through it (represented by the second diagram) and said that's what he'd like to be and thought it was pretty ideal. Then he drew another line and said that was me (represented by the third diagram) . . . That's what people thought of me there (always up). No one has said that to me–all through high school, all through college. What it means to me now is that I'm finding new worth in myself and I'm really happy with myself. I really don't know why. I guess after a year and a half, I wanted (my girlfriend) to be married. It was like a great burden lifted from me–almost.

Wherever I went in France, I was complimented on my accent, which was a result, I believe, of both regular use of the language lab in New Haven, but also imagining myself as an actor, pretending to be a Frenchman. (To this day, I think that's an important aspect of learning another language.)

The biggest compliment I received was from a young lady I asked to dance in a pavilion on the beach in Sète on the Mediterranean where we spent weekends, when she said, "Tu es très sympa." I could now go home and face senior year.

Before I could get back to New Haven, however, I faced one more adventure in London. I took a twenty-eight hour train trip from Rome to London and

. . . As I stood in Victoria Station wondering just what to do next, a guy came up to me and asked me if I was a musician (I have been toting my guitar around) and (if I) wanted (to rent) a room for 2 pounds a week. This was a present from heaven actually, (since I had practically run out of money), and the upshot of it all is that I'm staying with three members of a British pop group The Riot Squad. They're really sort of fun. Last night I went with them to a booking in a pub. Amazing show. The first half was complete with paper flowers and hippie clothes, but the second show was almost unbelievable. I like their music and their lead singer was great, but they came out with their faces all painted, almost like clowns and with the stroboscopic lighting and paper flowers and loud guitars, it was quite a weird show. But I went back to the dressing room after and you wouldn't think they were the same group that was carrying on so wildly on the stage. They were quite subdued, discussing the audience and the songs and things. It was really interesting.

The lead singer was David Bowie who had just joined the group in early 1967.

Chapter 13 – Senior Year

NOTE: Recall Lanny Davis' comment that "Dink Stover's fabulous career is followed no further than the end of his junior year, since author Owen Johnson bestowed on his hero the supreme accolade: a tap from 'Bones'. There was simply no need to continue the narrative, for any further achievement would have been anti-climactic." Accordingly, there will be no further citations from Johnson's book.

Senior Year

Senior year. What can I say about senior year? Surely, it was the shortest and gladdest year of the "shortest, gladdest years of life."

I decided in the fall to eliminate competitive gymnastics from my daily routine and that included giving up being a cheerleader. This was intended to give me breathing room to enjoy my senior year as much as possible. It might be said that my decision paved the way for my classmate George W. Bush to become a cheerleader, an activity he took on with such enthusiasm that he was arrested for attempting to tear down the goalpost after Yale clinched the Ivy League title at the Princeton game that year. I would learn later in law school that there was insufficient nexus or causality between my act and his to warrant my being held liable as an aider or abettor.

I was expecting a crushing workload in my courses, since I needed to cram in a variety of art history courses in order to complete the major in time to graduate. So, I signed up for the final studio art course of my career–calligraphy–as a load lightener. (I really was interested in calligraphy!) That turned out to be the most important decision of my entire life.

The course was a requirement for the graduate school in graphic design and was therefore populated with young women graduate students, the only class I took in four years with women. It was also the only class where the professor called role, announcing my name daily along with the others in the class.

I took the class with my good friend in Morse College and, as seemed natural at the time, we ranked the women on a scale from 1 to 10. The girl whom I ranked as No. 1, Louise Klingel, later turned out to be my wife of now over forty years. Irony of ironies! Three weeks later, hearing my name daily, she came up to me and said, "Did you have an older brother at Stanford?"

They had dated. Purely platonic, I was told. No matter. She was fun to be with. I liked fun. It worked. Well.

We dated regularly, Louise and I, over the next several weeks. She used my dorm room as a parking place during the day between classes, since it was a long haul from her apartment on Prospect Street to the campus, so we saw each other regularly. I was increasingly impressed with her bravery in leaving Palo Alto where she had been a Stanford undergraduate and had won the art prize on her graduation. She had had a good job in Palo Alto and she loved California, but she gave it up for the "opportunity" to come to New Haven to enroll in Yale's graphic design program. She had real talent and Yale was the place to nurture it.

The fun continued at the Christmas break. I invited Louise home to Detroit, where the Whiffenpoofs were scheduled to give a concert. After driving all day and most of the night, we arrived at my home in the middle of the night and went immediately to our assigned beds. My older brother–the one who had dated Louise–arrived at home later in the middle of the night and went immediately to his assigned bed. Well . . . You can imagine his surprise when, in the morning, he came down to breakfast only to find Louise had beaten him to the breakfast table. He rubbed his eyes and asked incredulously, "Did I invite you here?" In the absence of the Internet and cheap long-distance phone calls, no one had bothered to tell him we had met.

We went back to New Haven early to enjoy the campus without the pressure of classes. Besides, we had a project in calligraphy that was due on the resumption of class. Life was grinding on with my heavy course load in art history, but the reality of the Vietnam War was settling in.

Fall turned into winter; winter turned into spring–the spring of 1968.

Books would be written about this period with startling titles such as *1968: The Year that Changed the World*, published by Time Inc., and *1968: The Year the Dream Died* by journalist Jules Witcover describing a world gone crazy. Riots erupted everywhere, cities burned and students occupied university administrative buildings on the campuses of Columbia University and the University of California at Berkeley. Shocking events took place one after another. The Tet Offensive heightened the intensity of the war effort, as well as the protests against the war. Dr. Martin Luther King, Jr. was assassinated in April and later in June Senator Robert F. Kennedy was gunned down during his campaign for the presidency of the United States.

The draft was on everyone's mind. Volunteering for the military did not have the aura of patriotism that it had in other eras. I had completed my plans to attend Columbia Law School and was prepared mentally to take on that task. I determined to go ahead with my plans and let fate deal me another hand if that was meant to be. I had torn a knee ligament in high school, the result of a skiing accident, leaving me with a loose joint, and I had a hunch that might keep me out of the draft. Time would tell.

Thoughts of a Senior

I continued to be haunted by the demons of the last two years. I wrote in the early fall:

> Saw (my girlfriend and her husband) (They were married the previous summer.) Saturday night at Mory's. It just destroyed me. I couldn't look at her. She walked right next to me. I could hardly hold my drink after I sat down. It made me so nervous. I wish I could stop feeling that way. She set such a terrible precedent for anyone to follow.

Midway through senior year, I was moved to write some thoughts on my Yale experience.

> What is overwhelming to me has been the value that I place, and have placed, on being at Yale. I cannot put into words what being here has meant to me. I have lived and died here so many times during the past three years and in the presence of such greatness that I am very, very proud to feel such a part of Yale. I have gone to sleep at night innumerable times thanking God for the good people I'd been with, the amazing and wonderful things that happened to me here, the intense satisfaction with my work–yes–the fact that I got to do it. I've found great worth in myself and in those people. That never happened to me before. Mr. Fischelis once showed me a letter he received from Adlai Stevenson after working with him in the 1952 election. He described the personal satisfaction he'd gotten.

> An example: while studying for Scully's final in June, (Lloyd) struck up a conversation with me as we studied the photo exhibit. We wound up studying two solid days together. (Lloyd) was a Whiff, a Phi Beta Kappa and decided last November he didn't want to go to medical school and was accepted hands-down at the Yale Law School. He's also one of the most real, sensitive, alive human beings I've ever met. He once planned

to be an architect and with another Whiff designed a secret society. He has a sense of beauty and rightness in the world around him. You've got to hear him sing *Quiet Girl*. He helped *me* study. I gave *him* help on some of the reading.

There's more. Tonight I was doing a lettering project. I did a paragraph he wrote for the Whiff album describing the Whiff experience–trials, tribulations and worth–on a poster in uncial letters. Three guys came back from the movies and told me with dropped jaws that it was the best thing they'd seen either Seth or me do all fall and shouldn't I give it to (Lloyd) or to Mory's for the Whiff room to be framed on the wall.

It may be silly and not work but Monday I may take a trip to see the manager and see if I can sell him on the idea. Things like this make being alive worthwhile.

I see (Lloyd) occasionally. He told me last week he was engaged to the girl whose picture he'd shown me in June, did I want to come to Yale Law, not to worry about senior-itis or first-year law school–that you have to live, too. Things like all this are some of the most important things I'll carry away from Yale–and that was only typical. On top of that, add the confidence that I *can* be in the top 7 percent of my class *here* if I shut out enough of the world–I *did*. But I have such (great) friends and met such (great) people . . . And in fact it's these kind of people I want to work with the rest of my life.

In the study of psychology, the term "transference" has been taken to mean a phenomenon characterized as the redirection of feelings and desires, and especially of those unconsciously retained from childhood, toward a new object. There is evidence of this in a later letter I wrote:

I take great comfort in my friends here–and they're a wonderful group. And when people ask me where I'm from– as they did in France–I say "New Haven". I was elated to be coming back here where my real world is. Everything here is what I hang on to and I love everything here with all the energy I used to expend on (my girlfriend). It's all I have, so there are times when I'm very happy with the world I live in here, but all the while I know it's because it's a surrogate for what I am now missing and must eventually find again.

By early April, normalcy began to creep back into my life. With perhaps unwitting insight, I wrote to my parents:

Thanks for (sending my tennis) racquet. Played with Louise last Sunday. She hits really well actually and we really had fun on a cool Sunday morning . . . we're going to be playing quite a bit, I think . . .

Behind these thoughts was a plan for Louise and I to marry a year after graduation. The plan was proposed with the delivery from Tiffany's in New York of Louise's engagement ring at Thanksgiving following graduation.

The proposal was accepted.

Thereafter, my parents travelled to Minneapolis to meet Louise's parents. During a tour of their home, my mother clasped her hand to her mouth and exclaimed, "My God, that's me!" At Louise's graduation from Stanford, her father had taken her picture (later enlarged and hung on their wall at home) walking back from the stage with her diploma in hand. In the foreground of the picture were my parents, seated in the audience and there to witness my brother's graduation from Stanford.

The deal was clinched, giving new meaning to the phrase, "We *had* to get married."

Chapter 14 –
Law School

L aw school brought me to New York City, a common next step for many Yale graduates. After passing through New York on trips back and forth to New Haven for four years, I wanted to be in New York.

The first year I lived in the dorms on the Columbia campus on Morningside Heights. Louise continued with her graphic design program for its second year in New Haven and we got together on weekends one place or the other, planning to get married after first year. It was great fun to be able to go back to the Yale campus so easily, so much so that I even tried to transfer to Yale Law School. As with undergraduate transfer candidates, if there are ten applicants for each space initially, there are a hundred applicants for each transfer space–no chance. Love had to flourish in New York.

But first I had to deal with the draft. I was notified to report for my physical exam in Detroit in September my first year in law school. I had my exam switched from Detroit to New York, which took six months to accomplish. But there I was, trudging across the frozen tundra of the Columbia campus on a blustery March 1969 morning at 5:30 AM, the campus walls still stenciled with red-painted upraised fists, exclaiming the injustices of the previous spring. There were still student trials being conducted on the campus. I made my way in the dark down to the induction center at 39 Whitehall Street and spent the better part of the day chatting, but not glibly, with anonymous members of the Armed Forces, fear gripping my heart at each new venue where I was poked and prodded and tested from some new angle. The torn knee ligament was my saving grace–I was pronounced 4F. In October of that year, a bomb blast in the building, the consequence of protests against the Vietnam War, resulted in the closure of the Whitehall Station.

So, that behind us, Louise and I were married on a bright, sun-dappled day in June in Dwight Chapel on the Yale campus. My brothers joined me at the altar and Louise's best friends from Minneapolis and Stanford, along with my sister, were her attendants. In the pews was an equal number of Yale graduates and Stanford graduates, some of whom knew the bride and my brother, but didn't know me. However, it was almost like a family gathering. Drinks were drunk and toasts were toasted at the Yankee Silversmith in Wallingford, Connecticut.

The happy couple, after a night in the Plaza Hotel and a week in San Francisco, settled into married student housing at 112th Street and Broadway adjacent to the Columbia campus–an opportunity secured by the bridegroom, it is alleged, *before* proposing to his bride. While I might, if pressed, dispute the timing issue, it was a bit of fantastic planning, wouldn't you say? I thought so . . . Anyway, second year passed in relative comfort and we enjoyed being in New York, even without money.

We used to take snobbish pride in being able to get the Sunday *New York Times* at 11:00 PM on Saturday night. What we didn't read the night before, we took with us to read on a blanket in Riverside Park on Sunday afternoon, where, if you closed your eyes, the roar of the traffic on the West Side Highway sounded just like the ocean. You know, now I can't hear the ocean without thinking about the roar of the traffic on the West Side Highway.

Law school actually went by fairly quickly. One day was pretty much like another–a dizzying load of case reading, recitation in class (for better or for worse) and more dizzying case reading. Moreover, classes in the law school were taught using the Socratic method, a form of inquiry and debate, pitting opposing viewpoints against each other, based on asking and answering questions to stimulate critical thinking and to illuminate ideas.

In law school, I was taught for the first time to think. For example, I learned to question who made a certain statement, why he made it, what ideas are consistent with his statement, what ideas are inconsistent, would the author make a different statement if one or more changes were made in the facts underlying the statement. I had gotten through Yale memorizing things–French vocabulary, mathematical theorems and definitions, names and dates of artists and their works.

A different skill set, by the way, was required to take the bar exam which I did–successfully–in both Pennsylvania and, later, in California. For the bar exam, it was again necessary to memorize–this time as much black letter law as possible and then, on the exam, spot as many issues as possible in a set of facts to which the black letter law would apply and write out a description of those issues.

I studied for the two bar exams in completely different ways. In Pennsylvania, I went to the classes conducted by a commercial bar review company, took notes and tried to organize my notes into a coherent outline and then set about to master that outline. This I soon discovered that that was an inefficient way of commanding a vast body of material.

In California, I never went to class, but instead spent my time reducing the bar review course books to a few keywords that triggered in my mind various concepts in the black letter law. The course books were very well organized in both long form and short form outlines. These I reduced to a single page for each of a dozen course topics. By the time I had finished preparing for the exam, I could call to mind each of the single page summaries and I could write a coherent review of issues on the exam.

The Socratic method of learning the law is a tedious and time-consuming process, but I suppose it pounds into the student the process by which the law evolves in a democratic society. However, relying on it exclusively as a means for teaching law is, in my opinion, a mistake. It made me feel like a baby chick in a nest, beak open and arched skyward, waiting for food for thought to be crammed down the gullet.

It has been said that PhDs who do research look down their noses at medical doctors, because medical doctors are skilled at memorizing things, whereas research doctors don't want to memorize things they can look up in a book. Instead, they want to push the forefront of knowledge; but this view of skills ignores the fact that a medical doctor must command a vast body of material and recall it quickly to tend to the sick. Similarly, a lawyer must know the law in order to advise clients efficiently.

All in all, as an educational experience, law school paled in comparison to my undergraduate years. I felt as though I was very lucky to have stumbled onto Yale–and stumble I did, since the trip I took with my parents to interview schools in New England resulted in a chance encounter with the admissions officers at Yale whom I liked immediately.

Now, on graduating from law school, I thought it was important that high school students know what a great place Yale was.

Chapter 15 – Alumni Schools Committee

I had not been at Yale but six months when I heard the admonition: "You've been given a lot, and you're expected to give something back." This was the seminal thought behind both Yale's dedication to public service and my desire to tell high school students about Yale. It was my first opportunity to give something back.

So, after settling on a job with a law firm in Philadelphia, I set out to join the Yale Club of Philadelphia and to become a member of the Alumni Schools Committee. The ASC consists of Yale alumni devoted to the interviewing of students applying to Yale, as described in some detail in Chapter 1. The alum conducting the interview writes a one-page report to the Admissions Office answering the following four questions:

- To what extent will the applicant make a contribution to the Yale community?
- To what extent will the applicant benefit from the Yale community?
- To what extent does the applicant pursue things he or she is interested in?
- To what extent does the applicant make sacrifices to pursue things he or she is interested in?

I took this responsibility seriously and labored long over my one-page reports. After all, you held the future of the applicant to some extent in your hands. I always tried to minimize the importance of the interview when talking to an applicant, suggesting that its importance in the overall portfolio review was minimal, say 5 percent by weight, and this seemed to set the applicant's mind at ease.

I also advised the applicant that the interview was a two-way street, that I was there to give him information about Yale as much as I was there to give Yale information about the applicant. This turned the interview into a conversation, rather than a grilling, enabling the applicant to show his or her personality more easily.

Finally, while the interview was intended to be private, one-on-one, I always invited the parents to sit in for a final session to have their questions answered. I took the opportunity to do a little sales job on the parents who would be footing the bill, inviting them to call me if they had additional questions after the interview was over. I wanted them to think of me as a friend they could call on if needed.

The sales job usually revolved around financial aid, given the expense involved in today's Ivy League colleges. It always surprised parents to find that Yale's admissions policy was need blind, also described in Chapter 1.

Doing this, I became known as Mister Yale in the community. I believe people really appreciated talking to someone who seemed to be on their side–rather than sitting in judgment of the student and pontificating about whether or not the student was good enough to be admitted to Yale.

This difference in attitude on the part of the interviewer had other subtle ramifications. If the interviewer views his role as one of judging the student, then his judgment soon became sacred to him and he became vested with his opinion on whether the student should be accepted by the Admissions Office. "I don't understand why you didn't accept Johnny Smith. He was the most qualified candidate I've seen in ten years!" and "I haven't gotten a student into

Yale in five years!" were typical rallying cries from interviewers in the field to the admissions officers assigned to the region.

On the other hand, if the interviewer viewed himself as a kind of ambassador for Yale making information available about Yale to potential applicants—not recruiting, we don't need to recruit—so that students can make informed judgments about where they apply, then the interviewer can take greater satisfaction in his job of helping to find the right fit between Yale and a student.

Furthermore, the statistics of the admissions process leads to the conclusion that that is all an interviewer can hope for. With 80 percent of the applicants perfectly well qualified, second-guessing the process of choosing the class from the field was a futile effort.

On several occasions during the fifteen years that I worked on the ASC, we were given the opportunity in New Haven to review the entire admissions portfolios of ten or twelve student applicants. I never had an opportunity to review my own admissions portfolio, including the letters of recommendation from my teachers.

Armed with this kind of information, I attended college nights where I sat behind a card table and in front of a large Yale banner, chatting with whomever happened by and seemed even idly interested in attending Yale. I also developed relationships with guidance counselors in the local high schools, with knowledge and permission of the admissions office that they wanted us to penetrate those schools. The intent was to pick the counselor's brain about which students in the junior class were likely candidates for Yale for the next year, so we could begin talking to them. Again, we were not recruiting because we had no basis to do so, but rather opening their eyes to the prospect of applying to Yale.

This was very satisfying work and I served long enough to become Chairman of the ASC in San Francisco. As Chairman, I took it upon myself to get to know every member of the committee by having at least one telephone conversation annually. This was sufficient to get to know who really took the job of interviewing seriously and did it well. Of this group, I distilled those who by personality and predilection would be helpful in penetrating local high schools in the September through October timeframe, talking to seniors who were in the process of applying to colleges.

Again, we were not trying to drum up business for Yale but to deepen the dialogue between prospective applicants and Yale to increase understanding. This group of interviewers became known as the Alumni Schools Network and functioned as a subcommittee of the Alumni Schools Committee.

The idea of advance communication with high school students was refined to include developing a dialogue with juniors at high schools to further their understanding of Yale. In an Admissions Office newsletter, I wrote:

> How would you feel if you were a high school junior right now? It is April 1997, and your guidance counselor just invited you to a meeting with alumni representative from Yale who is coming to your school to talk to you about life at Yale. Of course, you would feel flattered . . . curious . . . anxious . . . excited! All of your senior friends have just heard from colleges, and the long process of writing applications and worrying over acceptances is almost over for them. You've wondered what it would be like for you when you begin that process in earnest next fall. Yale is coming to you – what a pleasant way to begin the college application process!

> This is the scenario the Alumni Schools Network (ASN) would like to have played out at public high schools and private secondary schools all over the country this May. The ASN will be encouraging Alumni Schools Committees throughout the US to assign at least one of its members to a local school for a meeting in May with juniors. At these meetings, arranged with the help of the guidance counselor at each school, the ASC member would conduct an informal presentation and discussion about Yale. The program would

make the (Yale) experience come alive for the students and would encourage their consideration of Yale in the fall.

Ideally, the ASC member would develop a long-standing relationship with the assigned school and its counselor, who each year would encourage top students to apply to Yale. By making information about Yale personally accessible to students, ASC members will be providing a valuable community service, helping students and their parents make informed decisions about the college search process. Yale also benefits from the increased visibility.

I can't resist telling a story that illustrates how the contacts with students before they apply to Yale work out in the real world. In another Admissions Office newsletter, I wrote:

I find myself describing the richness of Yale's musical traditions to high school students as part of my information development effort. To musically talented students, Yale affords an educational experience unmatched among liberal arts colleges and universities. To other students, like myself when I was undergraduate, Yale's music scene contributes strongly to the sense of community that is the hallmark of undergraduate life.

Late last December, I had a conversation with a member of the New Blue (Yale's first all-female a cappella singing group) who was home for the holidays. We were planning details for a Spring Sing in San Francisco involving three Yale singing groups on tour during spring break. Suddenly, she reminded me we had met many years ago. "Why, Mr. Casselman! Don't you remember? You gave me a tape of the New Blue five years ago when I was a student at Lick-Wilmerding High School."

Sometimes all the stars are properly aligned.

I do recall that, after talking to a student at a college fair, I went home and made a tape of the New Blue to send to the student. I suspect this small gesture had something to do with landing that student for Yale. I suspect, also, that the story of that gesture may have circulated among a few other students at Lick-Wilmerding High School. In any event, it was very satisfying to learn years later that the outcome was favorable for Yale.

These ideas were so appealing that, when the Dean of Admissions at Yale moved to Stanford, he took with him, and implemented at Stanford, both the idea of Alumni Schools Committee interviews and the idea of the Alumni Schools Network school visits in September, October and May.

One last story will illustrate the extent to which the Yale administration will go in helping a lost student, for convenience named Carlos, to find himself.

I received notice from the Yale Admissions Office that Carlos had applied to Yale and needed an interview for his admission portfolio. After a business meeting in the Central Valley, I stopped by his home in Tracy, California, where four boys and two parents lived. The parents barely spoke English after seventeen years in the US from their native Mexico. Carlos was clearly intelligent, articulate and soft-spoken but socially adventuresome, so I wrote a positive report and Carlos was accepted to Yale.

I visited Carlos while I was at the AYA Assembly in November of his first year. A tall lad, he was also bulky at 240 pounds, still wearing his high school varsity jacket with leather sleeves and wool body. I later discovered that he had been asked to leave Yale after his first year for inadequate academic performance. To continue pursuing his education, he attended classes at the University of California at

Berkeley, where he also took up crew. Yale acknowledged his efforts and he was readmitted as a sophomore after one year at Berkeley.

I next saw Carlos in the fall of his junior year. By then he had acquired a camel hair sports coat and proper shirt and tie, which he wore to our meeting. To my great surprise, he had shed fifty pounds, was still rowing crew, and had picked up an assignment doing research for a book written by a Yale Law School professor. If Carlos were lost in his freshman year, he certainly had found himself by his junior year.

What is most interesting to me was comment by the law school professor on these events. He said that Yale let Carlos down during his freshman year by not tracking him closely enough. (He needed a Bob Fischelis to comment on his work habits.) People with high raw native intelligence can lose the wind in their sails just as easily as anyone else.

Today, Carlos has been working at a law firm in California doing paralegal work and preparing to apply to Stanford Business School. We wish him good luck.

As Chairman of the Alumni Schools Committee, I was de facto a member of the board of the Yale Club of San Francisco.

Chapter 16 – The Yale Club of San Francisco

B eing a board member of the Yale Club of San Francisco opened up new avenues for involvement with the Yale community.

I was able to give vent to my interest in Yale music by conceiving of and then implementing the idea of a combined concert featuring both the Yale Whiffenpoofs and the Pacific Mozart Ensemble. The PME every year in the spring performed a pops concert that consisted of a cappella singing similar to the Whiffenpoofs. My thought was that, while the Whiffenpoofs attracted its own audience, we could hold a more significant event by combining the loyal audiences of both groups.

In performance, the two groups had obvious respect for each other. The event was so successful that we not only filled the Marines Memorial Auditorium in downtown San Francisco, but the combined concert was performed every other year for ten years, whenever the Whiffenpoofs came to the West Coast.

Stick around long enough, and soon someone will make you president. That was what happened.

Yale Clubs around the country have trouble getting and keeping both leadership and membership, except, perhaps, in major East

Coast cities like New York City, Boston, Washington D.C. and Philadelphia. In Kingman Brewster's democracy of "corporately defined success," where rewards were bestowed on those who scrambled to the top of the social and academic pyramid, such rewards "coerced conformity," in Brewster's words. In this atmosphere, Yale Clubs could flourish, since one's position in the pyramid could continue to present rewards in the real world after college, especially in the major cities where Yale graduates tended to flock pursuing careers in law, finance, business and government.

However, in the modern era, an individualistic, anarchistic definition of democracy has replaced open competition for corporately defined success as the standard, according to Brewster. In this era, for the undergraduate, and to a large extent for the graduate in the real world, success became "more related to effort and accomplishment and contribution to the College than it was to inherited status or to the machinations of a campus-wide political 'system.'"

The same sociological forces that affected campus success and career success also had an impact on the health of university clubs. The trend toward individual effort and accomplishment tended to diminish the rewards associated with position in the pyramid. University clubs became an adjunct to one's social life, indeed almost a sentimental adjunct, just one or two more cocktail parties during the year and a speaker from New Haven now and then. The world was becoming a matter of *what* you know, not *whom* you know. (Ironically, as the US economy has faltered in recent years, and Facebook and LinkedIn have provided electronic networking facilities to university clubs, Yale Clubs have experienced a resurgence in popularity.)

Without empirical evidence, it is hard to generalize as to why university clubs are not more successful. The only other university club I am generally familiar with is the Stanford Alumni Club. I have seen it function in Philadelphia, San Francisco and Santa Fe. In all three places, the level of activity was not high. An event would be scheduled, say a trip to Georgia O'Keeffe's home, and the turnout would be slight, mostly older people. My sense is that, without a regular schedule of events laid out well in advance, university clubs will continue to have troubles with membership and activity attendance shortfalls.

Furthermore, there has to be a condition or spirit around which alumni can rally. In many colleges, it is football that brings people together. At Stanford, it is the position of Stanford as the most exclusive and both intellectually and academically oriented university on the West Coast that brings its alumni together. At Yale, it seems to be community service and I think the founders would be proud of Yale's commitment.

The Yale Club of San Francisco was in decline when I was asked to be president. It was chronically short of cash since its membership rolls had fallen. Therefore, it could not hold expensive or risky events, further imperiling the Club with financial risk when it attempted to organize an activity. Without interesting activities, the Club could not raise cash. A vicious cycle ensued and threatened to overwhelm those still interested in sustaining the Club.

The first thing I did was to undertake discussions with the University Club about joint solutions to our common problems. The Yale Club of San Francisco had long held many of its events in the University Club, which had a wonderful facility at the top of Nob Hill. The University Club was planning a membership drive to offset dwindling revenues and quickly agreed to explore the prospects for joint events. We settled on a jointly sponsored squash tournament, pitting University Club players against Yale Club players. The University Club had a highly developed squash activity and a number of good players. The Yale Club had chutzpah. When the spilling of blood stopped finally, it was University Club Players 5, Yale Club Players 0.

Other benefits accrued to the position of President of the Yale Club. For example, I was appointed master of ceremonies for a traveling road show of professors and administrators from the University to various cities, including San Francisco as the first in a series dubbed "A Day with Yale in _____" (fill in the blank with appropriate city name). Also, when the medical school appointed a new Dean, I was the one to meet him backstage and introduce him to the assembled alumni.

I was beginning to feel a part of the University again.

Chapter 17 – The Association of Yale Alumni

The Association of Yale Alumni was formed in a series of meetings during the period from 1971 through 1972. Its constitution recites that its purposes are to

> ... help to maintain the stature of Yale University; to provide a channel of mutual communication between the alumni and the University and its Corporation; to oversee the direction of all alumni organizations and programs; and to provide the means (when appropriate) for the explication and forthright examination of University policies, in order that university position on basic issues affecting the University may be explained to the Assembly or its representatives and that appropriate recommendations may be advanced to the Corporation.

What is unusual about the AYA, and perhaps unique among American universities, is that it exists independently from the Development Office, where fundraising for the University is located. This independence allows the members of the AYA to function together to affect the direction of the University without regard to the burden of raising the billions of dollars necessary to run an institution like Yale. Thus, when an alumnus is approached by another on a matter of AYA business, he may greet his colleague as a friend, perhaps a new friend, rather than running in the opposite direction as a defense against an arm-twisting, fund-raising offense.

As a consequence of the structure, the AYA has become a complex but vibrant organization reflecting the intense but vibrant nature of the University itself. The constitutional mandate, together with the independence of the AYA, has permitted the AYA to become an important part of the governance of the University.

Service on the Association of Yale Alumni was where I really *became* a part of the University.

I spent three years as a delegate, representing my Yale Club, attending twice yearly Assemblies—one in November, coordinated with the Yale-Harvard Game, so that delegates could make a trip to New Haven doubly attractive, and one in April when spring is in the air and students are playing volleyball on the Cross Campus grass.

In the fall, I would take a red-eye flight from San Francisco overnight to New York, leaving at ten o'clock at night and arriving at five or six o'clock in the morning, and take a shuttle to New Haven, arriving at a hotel at eight o'clock in the morning. Throughout the trip, I would be half-asleep and at the hotel in New Haven grab another three hours of sleep.

On rising at noon, I would go outside to greet a brilliant fall day, crisp and cold, albeit long after the leaves have fallen in October. Every vista of the campus was filled with the quick intensity of students moving through their daily routines, stopping only to greet each other with enthusiastic delight.

Attending an AYA Assembly was like stepping onto a passing freight train; and the short walk to Rose Alumni House, which was called the alumni home away from home, was the first step onto that train. Registering in the Great Hall and gathering up the materials for the Assembly let you know where the train was going, if not how fast it was going there. A friendly chat with the staff member as I registered was the first indication of the train's speed. The second indication was likely to be a chat with an alumni board member who also arrived early to help prepare for the Assembly. By now, I was home.

Clutching my registration materials, and eager to take advantage of my free time this Thursday morning, I rushed out onto the campus to visit old haunts, perhaps sit in on a class or two, and generally absorb the flavor of student life. As a delegate, with no responsibility at the Assembly other than to report back to the Yale Club in San Francisco, I could enjoy the leisure, or participate in the frenzy, of being in New Haven. On Thursday night, I might have dinner with another alumnus or alumna or even a student I might have interviewed in the past. The evening might include a play mounted in one of the residential colleges, a singing group jamboree or a full-blown concert in Woolsey Hall.

On Friday, the real work of the Assembly began. Each Assembly was intended to highlight some aspect of Yale University, consisting of lectures, site visits and discussion groups, all staged to give delegates no more than 15 minutes break in between events, except at lunchtime when the luxury of 90 minutes allowed for lunch in one of the residential colleges and conversation with other alumni and, if you were lucky, with students.

Each session of the Assembly felt a little like being an undergraduate again—struggling to understand the assumptions behind the speaker's talk, the substance of the matter under discussion and the importance of the matter to you.

Friday evening was dedicated to cocktails and dinner in Commons, the huge, high ceilinged, dark wooded dining hall where all freshman take their meals. After dinner there was the awarding of the Yale Medal to four or five alumni for outstanding service to Yale. I was awarded the Medal in 2005. All of the names of previous winners attending the dinner are called out. In addition, the names of the winners are carved in wooden panels on the walls of Commons. Heady stuff.

Saturday morning was filled with getting up and getting ready for The Game. The bulk of that time was spent getting out to the Yale Bowl, a twenty-minute drive without traffic, and an hour on Game Day. The trek was rewarded with a tailgate brunch on the grassy playing fields surrounding the Bowl, complete with Bloody Marys and old friends. The particular tailgate we attend has been held for thirty-eight consecutive years, hosted by a Yale guy and a Harvard guy who became friends in the Navy and celebrate their friendship with this annual event.

The Game itself has been a yawner in recent years compared to that fateful day in the fall of 1968 when the two teams, both undefeated for the first time since 1909, met and came away tied for the Ivy League championship. That Game was heralded by the *Harvard Crimson* under the headline "Harvard Beats Yale 29-29" and chronicled in the movie of the same name. Harvard, down 29-13, rallied in the last forty-three seconds of the game to score two touchdowns and four extra points to tie the game. The movie has been called one of the best sports movies ever made.

As a result of Harvard's recent outstanding record against Yale, post-Game festivities are usually pretty subdued, often consisting of a drink at Mory's saloon, which *could* turn raucous given enough drink. At Mory's, enough was easily achieved through the injudicious use of silver loving cups, filled with alcohol, usually champagne cut with soda and a second designed to give the cup a color–for example, a Green Cup with crème de menthe or a Red Cup with grenadine. As tradition has it, once the first sip is taken and the cup passed around the table, it cannot touch the table until it is emptied and tested by turning the cup upside down on a white napkin. If the napkin shows any color at all (the cup was insufficiently emptied), the last to drink must buy another cup.

Dinner in any one of several restaurants in New Haven was very good after a round or two of cups at Mory's.

The relatively carefree days of the delegate soon gave way to service on the Board of Governors of the AYA. An elected position, membership on the Board of Governors carried with it responsibility to participate in the design and execution of Assemblies. It also meant attending meetings in New Haven four times annually, a pace of travel that has been reduced in recent years.

As a member of the Board of Governors, I actually got involved in helping to run the University, albeit in small ways.

I served on, and later chaired, the Alumni Fellows Nominating Committee, the principal purpose of which was to conduct due diligence reviews of individuals who had been nominated to serve on the Yale Corporation, the actual governing body of the University. Committee members would compile lists of people around the country familiar with the candidate and telephone those people, seeking information on the capabilities and other qualifications of candidates. We would then write reports on our findings that were to be used in the selection process.

I also conceived of and implemented a plan to utilize the best of the Alumni Schools Committee members to inform high school students about Yale, so that they could make informed judgments about where they applied to college, particularly to Yale. This development was the next major step in the crusade that began on graduation from law school and culminates with this book.

The plan, known as the Alumni Schools Network, is described more fully in Chapter 15. It received the endorsement of the AYA and became a major new development for the Admissions Office. It also earned me the *Iron Bulldog* from the Dean of Admissions, which adorns my desk to this day. The idea was so well received that, when the Dean left Yale for Stanford, and there implemented an interviewing process similar to Yale's, he also implemented the Alumni Schools Network idea.

As my six years as a delegate and board member drew to a close, I began to feel the way I felt in my senior year—that Mother Yale was about to boot me out of the nest. So, convinced that the best defense is a good offense, I decided to run for Secretary of the AYA, which would put me on a course to become Vice Chair and finally Chair of the AYA. In practice, the Secretary and Treasurer vie with each other to enter the Vice Chair-to-Chair track, so even if I won Secretary election, the future was still uncertain. If I made it onto that track, it would add a total of five years to the six years already served. More significantly, the Chair, who served a two-year term, had to be in New Haven every month for meetings at the AYA. That was too rich for my blood, too much to take on from San Francisco.

Still not wanting to be booted out of the nest, I ran for Secretary and won, earning one more year as an officer of the AYA after which I declined the privilege of continuing, effectively booting myself out of the nest. *Sic transit Gloria mundi.*

Chapter 18 – Community Service Summer Fellowship

The founding papers of Yale University called for a school "wherein Youth may be . . . fitted for Public employment both in Church and Civil State." The founders of Yale were ministers, concerned with the welfare of the community around them. If you believe, as I do, that organizations take on the personality of the people who lead them and that personality tends to perpetuate itself because leaders tend to hire in their own image, then you can understand how the commitment to public service might have lasted for the over three hundred years of Yale's existence.

Yale alumni activities reflect that commitment.

The Alumni Community Service Summer Fellowship places students in community service positions throughout the United States. These are paid positions, usually with non-profits, which permit students to have working relationships with alumni while developing an understanding of non-profits providing aid to the needy in the community. Housing is provided for participants who reside with a Yale host family. Participants are expected to provide their own transportation to and from work and their own meals, which was awkward if the student fellow was living with a family.

Each year, the CSSF Fellows were introduced and honored at an AYA dinner or lunch at the spring Assembly in the same manner that the Yale Medal winners are introduced and honored at the fall Assembly.

A 1995 transmittal from the AYA describes the goals and history of the CSSF program this way:

GOALS:
1. To enrich the educational experiences of students by adding community service fellowships to their summer programs, thereby adding to the general educational environment of the University.
2. To connect alumni and students interested in community service, providing them with the opportunity for dialogue.
3. To increase the awareness of local needs and to foster positive change for those in need in cities where Yale has alumni clubs/associations.
4. To extend this service activities of Yale clubs/associations by adding a community service focus to their other programs.

HISTORY

The AYA Community Service Summer Fellowship program provides Yale students with structured summer community service opportunities sponsored by Yale clubs/ associations . . . Yale Trustee Calvin M. Trillin '57 was an early advocate of the venture (based on his knowledge of the successful model in operation at the University of Notre Dame), and the idea was endorsed enthusiastically by the other Fellows of the Corporation. The financial generosity of Corporation member Frederick P. Rose '44E allowed the program to proceed without delay.

I had been embarrassed, while a delegate to the AYA, that San Francisco had not had a Summer Fellow, even though numerous other cities around the country had adopted the program. So I found a local private school, whose headmaster was a Yale graduate, which ran a summer program of enrichment education for talented students from poor school districts in Oakland.

This program, known as *Heads Up*, consists of sixty academically motivated seventh- and eighth-graders with financial need who attend math, science, English and study skills classes in the morning. The afternoon includes sports, student council, arts activities and self-esteem and group identity work. Working with a master teacher, a Fellow participates in both the morning and afternoon programs.

Sponsored by the local Yale Club, the *Heads Up* program resulted in one student spending the summer in housing provided by Club members and a stipend of $2,800 paid by the local private school where the student worked. The amount of the stipend is equal to the required summer earnings for students with financial aid obligations to the University, plus a small expense allowance. Sponsoring clubs must raise the entire amount of the stipend for each Fellow if the employer is unable to pay such amount.

From the standpoint of the student, the CSSF could be a lonely experience. If, as was the case, we had only one student intern for the summer, he or she had no colleagues with whom to share experiences or just hang out with – a flaw in the program that is corrected in the Bulldogs Across America program. See Chapter 20.

Louise and I found housing for the student, sometimes patching together multi-week house sitting assignments. It was difficult lining up these assignments and, of course, they had to be coterminous so that the student was not without housing even for one night. And, not only were house sitting opportunities difficult to arrange, but plans were always changing as families fine-tuned their vacation plans. As a result, the student intern would be continually packing up and moving to new quarters.

However, despite these drawbacks, the CSSF program provided

Louise and me with an opportunity to get to know current Yale students on a more intimate basis than the Alumni Schools Committee permitted and to learn more about life on the campus than even attending the AYA Assemblies. Finally, this effort brought San Francisco up to par with other cities in the United States in implementing a then currently popular community service activity.

Following is a description of several Fellowships that were implemented in various cities.

> *Boston* – Rosie's Place is a shelter and feeding program for mothers and children. Emergency and permanent housing are arranged as needed; casework and advocacy take place on an individual basis and involve contact with other agencies and programs. The Fellow, in consultation with the Director of Volunteers, will choose a summer project. The project may be group work with children, education programs for adults, recreation for families, or work with the existing volunteer network. The Yale Club of Boston will arrange housing which may be in one of Rosie's Place's permanent housing apartments.

> *Chicago* – The Alivio Medical Center provides primary health care services, preventative care and health education and training to Spanish-speaking families and individuals on the city's West Side. The Fellow will teach a health advocacy class to teenagers, will make individual job assignments at the Health Center to those students and will supervise the students as they learn with the larger community, develop job skills and become teenage health advocates.

> *Los Angeles* – Five Acres is a residential treatment and education center for abused children. Its programs include residential care, family-style group homes, a therapeutic

school, respite care, services for deaf abused children, home-based services and foster care training. Children at Five Acres are under eighteen years old and most have had an average of four prior placements; the goal of all Five Acres programs is family reunification when possible. Five Acres serves a multi-racial, multi-ethnic and multi-lingual population and the Fellow should be seeking that kind of setting. After training, the Fellow will work as a counselor with children in Residential Treatment and Family Group Homes.

Chapter 19 – Yale
Day of Service

Beginning in 2009, the AYA has sponsored a worldwide Yale Day of Service, where thousands of alumni all over the world dedicate one day to community service. It may be raking leaves, planting trees in a stream to prevent river bank erosion, painting the outside of a homeless shelter or some similar activity. The website for the Yale Day of Service describes the program this way:

> Yale alumni have an unparalleled tradition of service. From Dwight Hall's student-led community based programs to the highest levels of government service, Yale alumni have risen to the challenge to 'change the world,' and indeed many are doing just that as volunteers for Yale, or in their professional lives in the nonprofit sector, or by serving on boards of foundations, or as elected officials, or by giving of their intellect and creative energy to volunteer community projects.

The fourth global Yale Day of Service (was) held on May 12, 2012, with the goal that Yale alumni around the world (came) together on or around that day to serve their local communities. As in the past, this Day of Service serve(d) as a celebration of ongoing service by alumni and local Yale clubs as well as a catalyst for new service commitments . . .

(In 2012,) . . . over 3,500 members of the Yale community (volunteered) in nearly 250 sites in forty states and twenty countries. So much great work was done in soup kitchens, parks, homeless shelters, schools and more, all because members of the Yale community are committed to making a difference wherever they are. We appreciate the willingness of Yale alumni, family and friends to give their time and skills to local communities as they carry on Yale's great tradition of service as part of this important program.

In the spring of 2010, I mentioned to the President of the Santa Fe Watershed Association that the Day of Service was looming large in front of us. The result of that conversation was that half a dozen Yale alumni joined others in the community to plant 2,000 trees to help stabilize the riverbanks of the Santa Fe River.

As an aside, the President turned out to be a graduate of Harvard in 1968. We went together with our wives to a showing of the movie *Harvard Beats Yale 29-29*, the story of the infamous football game in the fall of 1968 where Harvard, behind by 16 points with forty-three seconds to go in the Game pulled up to a tie. With forty-three seconds left in the Game, when Harvard scored the first of two touchdowns, I shouted to the darkened theater, "OH, NO!" only to have him retort, "OH, YES !" To this day, we remain the closest of friends.

In subsequent years, Yale alumni from the Yale Club of New Mexico repainted the exterior of St. Elizabeth's Homeless Shelter in Santa Fe and cleaned the kitchen top to bottom.

In large ways and small, Yale has been true to its founding principle of service to the community. And Yale does it so well.

Chapter 20 – Bulldogs Across America

Dear Kirk,

Thank you so much for your dedication to ensure that we spend a fantastic summer--we had a phenomenal one! From dinners at your place (oh, your omelets are incredible) to Music on the Hill, horseback riding and mentoring us, you have offered us great opportunities while making us feel like we are at home in Santa Fe. I really appreciate it. We are going to truly miss Santa Fe, your welcoming smile and your adobe house. I enclosed a small souvenir that I got from Korea and it symbolizes an award/ID for those who get the first place in the merit-based national exam. Well, I just thought you won the first place in your dedication to the Bulldogs program as well as to Yale! Keep in touch Kirk, and I wish the best for all of your family. Thank you again and go Bulldogs!

Boola Boola, Andy
July 19, 2012

At the time I was winding up my presidency at the Yale Club of San Francisco, I had a call from the then Executive Director of the AYA inviting me to have conversation with Rowan Claypool, who had formulated and implemented a plan to create internships for Yale undergraduates in various cities around the country. Rowan and I sat down at a table at Mory's and two hours later I exclaimed, "What a great idea! No ego here. Just tell me what you want me to do and I'll do it!"

That was the birth of Bulldogs by the Bay in San Francisco.

BBB was the third program of eventually nine such programs around the country offering students the opportunity to work as a paid intern during the summer in a great variety of locations and types of work. Commencing with Bulldogs in the Bluegrass in Louisville, Kentucky, the program had by then expanded to Cleveland, Ohio. Both sites supported large programs with twenty to thirty interns each summer. After San Francisco, the program spread rapidly to Denver, Minneapolis, New Orleans, St. Louis, Houston and Santa Fe, all cities without large, established populations of recent Yale graduates. After founding Bulldogs by the Bay, my wife and I moved to Santa Fe, New Mexico where I founded Bulldogs in Santa Fe.

By then, alliteration had become an important aspect of the program, what with Bulldogs in the Bluegrass, Bulldogs by the Bay, Bulldogs on the Bayou, Bulldogs in the Big Easy. It seemed natural to call the Santa Fe program Bulldogs of the Butte, but it was deemed to be too easy for some comic undergraduate to distort the name into Bulldogs out the Butt, so we settled on what it was we had to sell, which was Santa Fe itself—a bucolic artist colony and cultural center in the middle of the high desert.

There is no better way to describe Bulldogs Across America than through the words of the Master, Rowan Claypool, as recorded in the Yale Alumni Magazine, July–August 2011 quoted at length:

(It all began with) an emerging sense that Louisville, like lots of heartland communities, was losing the best and brightest to places like Yale and needed a systematic way to regain them. There was not a Yale College graduate younger than thirty-five living in Louisville in the summer of' '99. There had been fourteen years of zero in-migration. Twelve years ago, this topic of brain drain in Kentucky was something that caused everybody to sort of sit up and say, 'Oh my gosh, how are we going to be a thriving economic engine if we're losing a significant portion of bright young folks?' I just dreamed up something to attempt to address it.

The structure of the program consists of four pillars: one is meaningful work. Two is the group experience. The third one is that we try to showcase how the community works behind the curtain, and the fourth is that each gets an assigned adult mentor–basically an adult who volunteers to befriend one of these kids.

As for the young Eli population today, (w)e've had at least 45 Yalies move to town and be gainfully employed at least a year. We've reversed the trend and made Louisville an attractive place to come after graduation. The brain drain was the reason to start it, but we found that there are other reasons to continue it. Each of the Bulldogs has a high likelihood of having a significant transformational experience during the summer. Yale would never have predicted this kind of program would be invented, and certainly not in Louisville.

(As for the program's growth,) (y)ou plant where the ground is fertile. It was fertile in Cleveland, it was fertile in San Francisco. You find alums who have a combination of civic interest and interest in Yale, and you give them a playbook. Roughly 10 percent of the Yale undergraduates are participating in the program before graduation. Last year a group of Yale undergraduates as big as the Davenport College applied. We're pulling them to places they never thought of spending their summer.

(Students are paid $2700 and get free housing, although) it varies from city to city. We've had something like 930 who've been across America, and something like 400 who've come to Louisville.

(One of the most meaningful moments was) (a)t the end of the summer of 2004, one of the students had a profound summer of finding herself. And she gave a speech about how, throughout the summer, I'm always showing up with watermelons.

I can bring a watermelon over in the evening, cut it out on the picnic table, and the Bulldogs will come out and eat. They wouldn't call me up and tell me how the day went, but if I show up with a watermelon, that way I get to know the group. I get to interpret the adult world for them. And I just enjoy watermelon.

(I've called Kentucky an exotic land, but) (w)hat is exotic? It's the thing that's unknown. Typical Yale undergraduates will know a ton about Europe and not a thing about Kentucky. If you go to Thailand, you're always in Thailand, but if you go to Kentucky, you have to develop a subtler ear for culture–because it's different, but it's your own country.

The Bulldogs program is a win-win-win-win.

The students win with a reasonable stipend and a terrific summer experience, dipping a toe into the real world of work and alumni activities that they will soon face. Both international students and domestic students need to be exposed to American cities and the American people far from New Haven, not just leaving them in an academic ivy tower. Domestic students often make decisions about their first job on the basis of very little information about the cities and regions to which they are applying for permanent positions and begin their careers. Moreover, the sustaining Ivy League professional networks of yesteryear no longer provide as many quality career opportunities to Yale graduates as they have in the past.

Bulldogs Across America helps to meet these needs of Yale with respect to both domestic and international students. In Bulldogs Across America, students get an exposure both to a variety of career opportunities and to alumni life, providing an in-depth view of American cities and the American people far from New Haven.

The employers win with a relatively cheap $10 per hour look at a highly qualified potential employee. The alumni win by having a highly rewarding activity involving young people from their alma mater. Finally, the University wins by forging meaningful links with its alumni. In the final analysis, the Bulldogs program is what universities *should* be doing for their students, alumni and community.

And Yale does it so well.

David Grant Noble '61 and interns at Tent Rocks, NM July 2012

Chapter 21 – Yale Career Network

J ust as Yale alumni are involved in the admissions process and the development of students through internships, so are Yale alumni involved with students after graduation as they give shape to their careers.

Recognizing this, the AYA set up the Career Counseling Resource Network, making it clear in minutes of the Club Committee on Career Services that

> . . . it is not a job placement service, but rather a service that disseminates career information to alumni through a club volunteer contact person. The career counseling volunteer discusses the career field and gives lists of people in a particular field who can give advice about a particular job . . . One of the purposes of the program was to link recent Yale graduates with their local Yale clubs . . . (The lists were to come from New Haven to be disseminated by the local club.)

I first became involved with career counseling at the Yale Club of San Francisco, which had a Career Counseling Committee but had not implemented the AYA program, as they had not implemented the

Community Service Summer Fellowship program. In the minutes of the Club board meeting dealing with that committee, it was suggested that the Committee post job offerings in addition to the informational interviews conducted by Yale Club volunteers. It was further suggested that it might be possible for the Yale Club to act as a clearinghouse for large companies that have job listings.

These suggestions provide insight into the reasons why career counseling organized at the local level didn't work – it was being organized to function as a headhunter organization or placement agent with false expectations on both sides, student and Club volunteer, as to what could be reasonably accomplished. The Yale Club members were primarily assigned to conduct informational interviews, probably to discuss the job climate and the process for obtaining a job. Inevitably, however, neither the interviewer nor the interviewee, as a practical matter, considered the Committee to be successful unless a job resulted. I myself felt that way whenever I did work for the Committee.

On the other hand, if we take a broader view of this activity, viewing it as a national activity, change the expectations and deploy some industry philosophy, career counseling can be a valuable activity for both the alumni and students.

A friend of mine in the headhunting business once explained to me how he worked. First, he placed a dot with his pencil in the middle of a piece of paper and he said, "That's you. Not to diminish you in stature, but that's you." Then, he drew a circle around the dot and said, "That's everybody you know." Then, he drew a second circle around the first circle and said, "That's everybody *they* know. Your next job is just two telephone calls away. You just don't know in which direction."

That was some of the best advice I ever received concerning job-hunting. A couple of stories will illustrate how this philosophy worked out in practice.

The night I received the Yale Medal for outstanding service to Yale, I sat next to a highly respected economist whose daughter was just six months out of Yale and having trouble landing a job in the entertainment industry in Los Angeles. Remembering that one of my classmates was a heavyweight entertainment lawyer in Los Angeles, I suggested that I could make a few calls and maybe be of some help. My economist colleague said, "No, no. You're not in the entertainment business and you're not in Southern California. You're in Northern California."

I called my classmate in Los Angeles. Though we had not spoken in several decades, he responded to my voicemail with his voicemail. "Kirk, how the hell are you?" The rest is history. He took the girl under his wing and corrected her pitch to potential employers. She got a job.

A second story: I had a call from friends whose daughter and son-in-law, both graduates of Yale, were looking to relocate from upper New York State to their native San Francisco Bay Area. Starting with the son-in-law, who was looking for a job in the alternate energy industry where I had spent a considerable number of years, I explained the dot and circles strategy and then set about to make a list of everyone in the industry I thought might be useful to him. The list consisted of people all across the country on the theory that networks and experience bases are national in scope and someone in Iowa may be able to recommend someone in San Francisco. He and his wife are now living in San Francisco.

I can't say that my efforts directly resulted in these alumni getting jobs. However, the effort rewarded me with renewed contact with old acquaintances, new contacts from each of them and the loyalty of the alumni I was trying to help.

Chapter 22 –
Music Program
for Graduates

I t is possible, upon graduation from Yale, to be involved with Yale music for the rest of one's life.

The outstanding Yale School of Music offers three graduate degrees, including a Doctor of Musical Arts. An anonymous donation of $100 million to the school permits all students accepted to the Yale School of Music to receive full scholarships–graduate school fully paid for. Established in 1854 and now one of the leading professional music schools in the world, the school has nurtured generations of successful performers, composers and cultural leaders.

Less academically formal, but more accessible to the bulk of students involved in music as undergraduates, is the Yale Alumni Chorus formed in 1997 as an experiment in international performance. In an unprecedented victory in logistics, 180 singers from 30 states made a successful two-week tour of China in 1998, appearing with some of the leading symphony orchestras in China. A second major tour took place in 2001 with a trip to Russia, Wales and England, again appearing with local orchestras.

However, what sets these tours apart is the involvement in outreach activities in each country visited. In China, the Chorus sang an exchange concert with extremely talented students at a local school and later shared a meal with the students, establishing themselves as "Ambassadors of Song". Since then, the Chorus has performed outreach concerts on five continents, consisting of both musical and social exchanges with local orchestras, choruses and schools with the mission to "build international understanding through the universal language of music." The Chorus co-hosted the Yale International Choral Festival in New Haven in June 2012 and will tour Lithuania, Latvia and Estonia in July 2013.

In the summer of 2010, Louise and I met one of the members of the Board of Directors of the YAC who invited me to sing with them on their next tour. *Mirabile dictu*–another opportunity to sing.

But, alas, too many moons have traveled the sky for me to try to contribute musically to the Yale Alumni Chorus.

Chapter 23 – YaleGALE

YaleGALE is the acronym for one of Yale's most ambitious projects in the international arena – the Global Alumni Leadership Exchange. The AYA describes YaleGALE this way:

> Yale is among the world leaders in alumni relations – it was the first college, in fact, to affiliate alumni by classes, to organize reunions, not to mention the first to organize a representative alumni association! Dedicated Yale volunteers have traveled the world at the invitation of other world leading universities to share their experiences in serving Yale as board members, reunion chairs, committee members and event organizers.

> Universities in the rest of the world generally do not have a culture of alumni stewardship; they receive the bulk of their operating assistance from governments. With no tangible reason to be engaged, their alumni are not compelled to provide for the next generation. With no underlying mission or reason to reconnect, they have not had reason to organize into class, club, school, or shared interest group affiliations. Through our YaleGALE exchanges, including conferences

in Istanbul, Beijing and Tel Aviv, we have broadened and enriched the alumni relations programs of many universities. In so doing we have further enhanced Yale's reputation around the world as a leader in promoting and strengthening higher education.

I have traveled with YaleGALE to Australia, Turkey, Scotland and England and I would guess that Yale is *the* world leader in alumni relations. None of the universities we visited seemed to have alumni associations as sophisticated as Yale's and all seemed quite interested in learning how our alumni association worked.

These trips were not to be mistaken for vacations. As it was with the AYA Assemblies, the days were tightly scheduled with meetings, presentations, discussion groups, lunches and dinners. The meetings, presentations and discussion groups were conducted by alumni who had been given assignments months before. The lunches and dinners provided an opportunity to meet with foreign alumni and administrators and more fully explore the ideas discussed in prior meetings.

A typical day would begin at 6:30 AM with breakfast and an organizational meeting at 8:00 AM, which would last until 9:00 AM. We were given detailed events for the day, but we also were given feedback from the AYA's officers and staff members on the previous day's meetings. We would then troop off to the next round of meetings, which would go until lunch with our hosts at the university. After lunch, we might take a walking tour of the campus or find ourselves in another meeting in the afternoon. Later, there would be drinks and dinner in one of the campus buildings. On other days, we might have several hours off to explore the town near the university. Dinner was almost always shared with our hosts and the day rarely ended before 10:00 PM.

We were always welcomed royally. For example, in Turkey the farewell dinner was held outdoors on the patio of a mansion five steps up from the Bosporus, also known as the Istanbul Strait, a waterway forming part of the boundary between Europe and Asia. We arrived at the mansion by boat, trees festooned with small, white lights twinkling and lighting the way. After dinner, we were regaled by exotically clad Turkish women dancing the horon.

In Australia and in Turkey, we took balloon rides– a quiet and gentle drift over spectacular terrain. In Turkey, we got a close-up view of the naturally carved stone sculptures at Cappadocia, where the only sound was the whoosh of the gas burner that accompanied the swift rise of the basket as it scraped over the rocks and then, with startling speed, ascended several hundred feet to provide a view of the plains below. In Australia, I learned to throw a boomerang under the careful guidance of two Australian teenagers.

In Australia, we were housed at home stays and were advised by the AYA to bring a present – something that was representative of where we lived. I chose to give a book about the American southwest written by Hampton Sides, a member of the Yale Class of 1984 who, by then, had written two books that had appeared on the *New York Times Best Seller List*. My goal was only to have him autograph the book for delivery in Australia. But in addition, he and his wife became our friends, adding richness to life and giving me new inspiration for writing this book.

The AYA has stated that the endgame of the YaleGALE exchange program is not yet clear but that relationships are budding all over the world. At a minimum, the name "Yale" and the quality of the Yale experience is becoming known all over the world. The endgame is suggested by the recent development of an agreement with the nation of Singapore to develop, at the sole expense of the Singapore government, a new university patterned after Yale. These developments are perfect examples of Yale practicing what it preaches in the willingness to take risks in support of education.

These vignettes illustrate how Yale transforms good works into good friendships all life long. And Yale does it so well.

Chapter 24 –
Reunions

C lass reunions at Yale are a big deal. Classes reunite on the campus every five years for a three-day convocation that literally repopulates the campus the weekend after the students leave for home in May. So popular are these long events, sponsored by the AYA, they must be held on two separate weekends to accommodate all who wish to attend. All classes whose graduation year ends in the same digit (e.g., 1968, 1978, 1988, etc.) celebrate reunion together and together with classes whose graduation year ends with the digit five years later (e.g., 1973, 1983, 1993, etc.).

Each class is housed together in one of the residential colleges. Some elect to stay in hotels adjacent to the campus because, in truth, you have to be willing to rough it by staying in the college. The rooms are clean – broom clean – but populated by only the barest of essential furniture – bed, desk and chair, with an occasional orphaned couch. There was at least a hint of elegance in the bath towels supplied, rolled and placed in the shape of a "Y" on the bed.

Some might think of this as Jail, not Yale, and so they escape to the local hotels. However, living together, sharing bathrooms and crossing paths with classmates served to deepen the sense of coming home. And it is distinctly reminiscent of the first and last days in the college, a poignant reminder of the breadth and depth of the experience we had at Yale.

The AYA Class Officers' Handbook describes Yale reunions as follows:

> The most effective way to strengthen ties among classmates, and between classmates and the University, is to bring the class back to the Yale campus. Over the course of these three- or four-day programs, classmates have the opportunity to rediscover you and to learn how the changes over the years have allowed the University to remain true to its mission . . .

> Class reunions may be held in either the spring or fall, each having distinctive advantages and disadvantages . . .

> **Spring Reunions**: . . One of the most attractive features of a spring reunion is that each reunion class is assigned to one residential college or the Old Campus. These facilities serve both as headquarters and home base for the class during the reunion weekend. Classmates have the option of taking rooms on campus in the college; meals are served in the courtyard under a tent or in the dining hall; refreshments are available in the college throughout the weekend.

> **Fall Reunions**: Dates for fall reunions are determined by the reunion class . . . typically scheduled to correspond with home football weekends. Fall reunions are special because classes have a chance to return to Yale when the University is in session. Classmates have the opportunity to audit classes, attend concerts and see theatrical performances, take meals with current students and faculty, and revisit those activities that were important to them as undergraduates. Rose Alumni House serves as headquarters for fall reunion classes, and remains open throughout the reunion weekend for use by the class. The Great Hall functions as a common area where reunionees can relax, visit with classmates and enjoy refreshments.

Like the AYA Assembly, lectures, tours and discussion groups are the meat of the reunion program, except it is the members of the class who put on the program. People generally adopt the right spirit for these events, being both interesting and interested, as anyone who is predisposed to attend a reunion is likely to be. And well they might be, since discussion groups included some of the most interesting people in our class dispensing the wisdom of our age.

I think it's fair to say that most reunionees come to reunions to visit with old friends and to relive some of their fond memories of Yale, much as they might appreciate commentary by their classmates on the state of the world.

But perhaps even more important than reuniting with old friends is the meeting of new people who become new friends. This is true not only within a particular class, but among the other classes sharing the reunion space and time. Some of my most enjoyable conversations about the Yale experience have been with members of the Class of 1938.

Recently, Louise and I attended a Stanford reunion, which lacked the intimacy of a Yale reunion. The residential college environment was far more conducive to conversation. While Stanford has lengthened its reunions from a cocktail party after a football game to a two- or three-day event, it stages a lunch or dinner or panel discussion, which reunionees attend but then disappear into Stanford's huge campus. At Yale reunions, the residential college courtyards remain set up for conversation throughout the weekend and serve as focal points for conversation both among classmates and between members of neighboring classes.

I hesitated to mention my classmate Dick Brodhead's comment at our last reunion, but I ultimately overcame my hesitation. He said that we appeared to the students then on campus the way the Class of 1923 appeared to us when we were students at Yale.

Frightening.

REGISTRATION AND CHECK-IN take place at Class Headquarters in Dwight Hall on the Old Campus. Headquarters opens at 10:00 a.m. on Thursday, May 27, remains open 24 hours a day, and closes at 2:00 p.m. on Sunday, May 30. Undergraduate Reunion Clerks are available to provide assistance and information all weekend.

FREE PARKING FOR THE CLASS OF 1968 is available at the Pierson Sage garage (Traveling north on Whitney Avenue, turn left at first light beyond the Peabody Museum). A shuttle bus will run between the garage and the campus all weekend. After 5 p.m. on Friday, all Yale lots are available. Please do not park on the street, as parking regulations are strictly enforced. You will not need your car during the Reunion Weekend.

CLASSMATES STAYING IN HOTELS should park at their hotels.

MANY ACTIVITIES HAVE BEEN PLANNED by the Association of Yale Alumni for the enjoyment of all. The AYA will provide a pamphlet titled <u>Events for All Reunion Classes</u>, and some of its listings are duplicated in this Class Program. You are also invited to visit Rose Alumni House (232 York St.) during the weekend.

<u>THURSDAY, MAY 27</u>

10:00 a.m. and all day	Registration begins at Reunion Headquarters in Dwight Hall on the Old Campus.
	Lunch on your own. A guide to New Haven restaurants is available at Headquarters.
	See AYA schedule for afternoon tours.
6:15 - 7:15 p.m.	Cocktails at the tent on the Old Campus.
6:30 - 8:30 p.m.	Italian Buffet for classmates and families in the Old Campus tent.
9:00 p.m. - 1:00 a.m.	Conversation, music and refreshments under the tent.

<u>FRIDAY, MAY 28</u>

7:30 - 9:30 a.m.	Breakfast in Commons.
9:00 a.m.	*<u>AYA Faculty Lecture</u>. "An Unhappy Family: the Interaction of Judaism, Christianity and Islam." John E. Boswell, A. Whitney Griswold Professor of History. Art Gallery Lecture Hall, High Street entrance.

Document1

Typical reunion schedule

10:00 a.m. *AYA Faculty Lecture. "Where's the Revolution? Thoughts on China Today." Jonathan D. Spence, George B. Adams Professor of History, Chairman and Director of Graduate Studies, Council on East Asian Studies. Art Gallery Lecture Hall, High Street entrance.

11:00 a.m. *AYA Faculty Lecture. "What's Killing New Haven?" Douglas W. Rae, Elizabeth and Varek Stout Professor of Social Sciences, Professor of Political Science and Professor at the School of Organization and Management. Art Gallery Lecture Hall, High Street entrance.

12:00 - 1:30 p.m. Buffet luncheon on the Old Campus. University Commons in case of rain.

2:00 - 3:00 p.m. "The University and the Public Forum." Special 1968 lecture by Jaroslav Pelikan, Sterling Professor of History. Professor Pelikan has been on the faculty since 1962 and is an enormously popular lecturer with students and alumni alike. Law School Auditorium, 127 Wall Street.

3:30 - 5:00 p.m. "The Class of 1968: Where Were We Then, Where Are We Now, Where Are We Going?" Class Panel featuring Richard H. Brodhead, Robert K. deVeer, Jr., Randall S. Fredrikson, James E. Ponet, Ronald G. Rosenbaum, Derek Shearer and Strobe Talbot. Law School Auditorium, 127 Wall Street.

5:45 - 7:15 p.m Cocktails under the tent on the Old Campus.

7:30 p.m. Class Banquet in University Commons. Presentation of Class Gift to President Howard R. Lamar, and remarks by the President.

After dinner, move to Woolsey Hall for a concert by the Whiffenpoofs of 1968 and our own Glee Clubbers.

10:00 p.m. - 1:00 a.m. Refreshments and dancing at the tent with music of our era provided by The Boomers, featuring our own Richard Gould '68, The Uptown Horns and Miss Dynomite and the Vicious Bitches.

Document1

Typical reunion schedule

7:30 – 9:00 a.m.	Buffet breakfast in Commons.
9:15 – 10:30 a.m.	"'68 in the Movies: A Light-hearted Look at the Cinema." Classmates Peter J. Dekom, Lloyd Kaufman, Steven Kovacs, Peter F. Markle. Art Gallery Lecture Hall, High Street entrance.
9:00 a.m.	*College Admissions and Financial Aid. Discussion with Richard H. Shaw, Jr., Dean of Undergraduate Admissions and Financial Aid. 102 Linsly-Chittenden Hall.
9:30 a.m.	*AYA Faculty Lecture. "Art and Sport in the Black Atlantic World." Robert Farris Thompson, Master of Timothy Dwight College and Professor of History of Art. Law School Auditorium, 127 Wall Street.
9:30 a.m.	*Undergraduate Life at Yale College: A Student Panel. 101 Linsly-Chittenden Hall.
10:45 a.m. – 12:00 noon	*Education at Yale College, Today. Faculty panel moderated by President Howard R. Lamar.
12:00 – 5:00 p.m.	Class Family Outing at Holiday Hill. Lunch and a wide variety of recreational activities are available (bring your own tennis equipment, swimming suits and towels). The outing will take place rain or shine, as Holiday Hill has ample indoor facilities in the event of inclement weather. Shuttle buses will start leaving from High Street Gate at 12:00 noon and run until 5:00 p.m.
4:00 p.m.	*AYA Faculty Lecture. "The Relentless Pursuit of Knowledge -- and Its Limitations." Jaroslav Pelikan, Sterling Professor of History. Art Gallery Lecture Hall, High Street entrance.
6:00 – 7:15 p.m.	Cocktails at the tent, Old Campus.
7:30 p.m.	Dinner in University Commons.
9:30 p.m. – 1:30 a.m.	Dance at the tent to the music of Nik and the Nice Guys, with a special appearance by Martha Reeves and the Original Vandellas.

(see over)

Document1

Typical reunion schedule

NUTTER, McCLENNEN & FISH

ATTORNEYS AT LAW

ONE INTERNATIONAL PLACE
BOSTON, MASSACHUSETTS 02110-2699

TELEPHONE: 617 439-2000   FACSIMILE: 617 973-9748

CAPE COD OFFICE
HYANNIS, MASSACHUSETTS

ROBERT H. BAKER

(617)439-2259

June 4, 1993
99980-0048

Kirk J. Casselman
1121 Winsor Avenue
Piedmont, CA 94610-1048

Dear Kirk:

I just want to put into writing my heartfelt thanks, which
I already conveyed to you orally, for your tremendous job in
puting together the singing groups. I think for many people
the singing was the highlight of the Reunion. I know I
certainly enjoyed it. I have been humming the Whiffenpoof Song
all day long (maybe it's my subconscious Freudian desire not to
let my brain get back into the humdrum of work). You put a lot
of effort into organizing everything, and I very much
appreciate it.

I gather that you and Louise come to Boston periodically to
see Jon and Liz Steffensen. I hope that on your next trip you
can visit with Sue and me as well.

Thanks so much again!

Sincerely,

William H. Baker

WHB/amc

7449q/3

Reunion thank you note

133

Chapter 25 –
Reunion at the
White House

A h yes, then there was the reunion at the White House.
One in our midst had been elected President of the United States.

The date was Thursday, May 29, 2003.

The invitation read, "The President and Mrs. Bush request the pleasure of your company at a picnic dinner in celebration the 35th Reunion of Yale '68 to be held at the White House on Thursday, May 29, 2003 at six o'clock Entertainment by the Yale Whiffenpoofs of 2003, the Yale Whiffenpoofs of 1968, The Baker's Dozen The Visitors Gate 15th St. and Pennsylvania Avenue NW"

Needless to say, journalists had a field day, discussing Bush's fear at Andover that he would not be accepted at Yale, his opinion as a Texas politician that Yale was an incubator of intellectual snobbery and his incipient rapprochement with Yale. Bush had been angered by Yale's failure to grant an honorary degree to his father until 1991.

Bush's love-hate relationship with Yale had been ameliorated when, four months into his term, he was granted his own honorary degree and it was further improved by the acceptance of his daughter

Barbara as an undergraduate, extending the Bush legacy well into the millennium from its origin with James Smith Bush (Class of 1844) and including in the 1920s George W. Bush's grandfather, Prescott Bush.

Although not as large as the parties thrown by the Clintons at the White House, the event nevertheless was well attended. 950 invitations yielded 600 attendees.

Shortly thereafter, there was a wonderfully insightful piece published in the Yale Alumni Magazine by Steve Weisman '68, then chief diplomatic correspondent for the *New York Times*:

> It seemed fitting, somehow, that the week before the reunion of the Class of 1968, the celebration began in the comic strip *Doonesbury.*
>
> "Can you believe our rush chairman invaded *Iraq?*" asks a drunken Old Blue. Upon being informed that his fraternity brothers have arrived at the White House, the president tells an aide, "Cordon them off. I'll be right there."
>
> As it happened, at the Class of 1968 reunion festivities on May 29, President Bush's classmates had unlimited access to our host—if you could get past the crush of people around him—as well as free run of the White House, from the East Room to the Rose Garden, where you could peek into the Oval Office. Tables and chairs were set up throughout the main floor, but most people spent their time roaming the area and soaking in its history.
>
> The next day we boarded our own Hogwarts Express, a chartered train that left from Union Station in Washington for New Haven and another two days of reunion celebrations. Thirty-five years ago, a four-and-a-half-hour train ride with several hundred members of our class would have taken a toll on our livers. For us over-the-hill guys—"I didn't know

we were supposed to bring our fathers," one of my classmates said—the fizz was more Perrier than Budweiser.

The President of the United States was in better physical shape than most of us. But of course George W. Bush has time to work out and jog every day, a luxury most of us don't have. His hospitality insured that, as the largest gathering of our class since graduation, the reunion was a resounding success. Classmates who had never been to a reunion came to this one, and the White House was aglow with nostalgia, humor, warmth, and yes, a little bit of incredulity.

It was also fitting that the evening was preceded by some soul-searching. More than a few classmates vowed not to go, in private protest against the war in Iraq or other policies. If the anguish was a little self-important, it must be said that our class has always been a hotbed of self-importance. We are, after all, the Class of 1968—graduated in a year that, as Ron Rosenbaum wrote in our 25th reunion class book, was "different from all other years." We were the first Baby Boomers, born after the 20th century's worst apocalypses. We came of age in an era of cultural and political revolution. When we were seniors, *Time* magazine made the members of our generation its "Man of the Year." And who did they put on the cover? A member of our class! (He was snapped by a photographer looking for emblematic faces in front of the Yale Co-op.)

With great respect to my classmates, my own feeling is that George W. Bush did more to honor our class than we did to honor him. No denying that we are a diverse and cantankerous lot, and yet each of us was made to feel welcome. For a couple of hours, the president and Mrs. Bush stood and greeted everyone in a receiving line. The president then spent another few hours of mingling, autograph-signing, picture-taking, hugging, and laughing. There were no speeches, only a presentation by the Whiffenpoofs of a plaque, two bulldogs, and an honorary membership in Yale's most celebrated singing group. The Whiffs confer nicknames on their own, a time-honored tradition; the newest member's was "Fermez La" Bush. (The nickname may or may not have something to do with the fact that, as Bush acknowledged, he can't carry a tune. A real Whiff later said the admission was an understatement.) With their arms around each other's shoulders, Bush and his Whiffenpoof classmates joined with everyone else in rousing versions of "The Whiffenpoof Song" and "Bright College Years," waving napkins and all.

What was most striking was that President Bush seemed to be enjoying himself as much as his guests were. It was the biggest party he had thrown as president and, according to security people, bigger than anything thrown by his party-animal predecessor. When it was all over, we went off into the night, many of us heading toward New Haven in the morning. Our host headed toward Poland, Russia, France, and the Middle East. One classmate had said to him, "You must be under so much pressure." He shrugged and looked nonchalant, as if the course were a gut. Well, OK, maybe it is hard to believe he invaded Iraq. But for one memorable evening, it all made absolute sense.

In the shadow of a great journalist, I will add my own commentary.

First of all, a college reunion at the White House is not about politics. It's about history. It's about government. It's about freedom. It's about friendship. It's about experiencing the world and about any one of a number of other aspects of being alive. Now admittedly, it is true that a number of classmates wore pins on the underside of their lapels that read *Yale '68 Loyal Opposition*.

Second, while I did not know President Bush as an undergraduate (he successfully avoided the intermediate step of performing on the gymnastics team on his way to becoming a Yale cheerleader), my best friend in both college and law school, who was in Skull and Bones with Bush, defended him as a loyal friend and sensitive human being. He had been to every inauguration of Bush and told many humorous stories illustrating Bush's personality. I conclude that Bush is a man who knows his limitations and his legacy advantage, but who, over many years, developed aspects of his being to maximize his effectiveness as a person. In a balanced assessment of Bush, you have to respect that.

Third, even my wife, who was as opposed to Bush's politics as anyone in the room, admitted that he was a gracious host that evening and that he exhibited charisma she had not expected.

Finally, the train ride back to New Haven from Washington, DC was a unique opportunity to run into people I may have talked to briefly on the phone but never met. The idea was a stroke of genius; it added a whole new dimension to the weekend.

Loyal opposition button

The author and President George W. Bush

Chapter 26 – In Summation

For our twenty-fifth reunion, the Yale Class of 1968 published a hardbound book containing essays by members of the Class, which by design were intended to explore reflections about our lives in the prior twenty-five years. Responding to that call, I wrote the following essay, which I think will serve as a summation of the principal topics in this book.

You asked for reflections about my life in the last twenty-five years. What has mattered to me? What may lie ahead? At the time of our twenty-fifth reunion, I cannot help but direct my reflections toward my years at Yale and their meaning to me now. I've developed these thoughts over twenty years work with the Alumni Schools Committee talking to students about my experience at Yale and listening to reports of their experience there.

Liberal Arts Education—the purpose of a liberal arts education, and I believe the whole point of being alive, is to pursue those things for which you have interest or talent. There may be times when you lose interest in things for which you have talent and times when you become interested in things for which you have no talent. To realize your potential as a human being, you have to explore both interests and talents, in spite of the clear risk that you won't necessarily "succeed" in some endeavors. To miss the opportunity to stretch yourself as far as possible is much more disappointing, even tragic, than not to have succeeded. A liberal arts education teaches you how to live, not how to make a living, so Yale taught me to take risks and to savor the results, positive and negative, as a vital part of the human experience

Intensity–Intensity is a hallmark of the Yale experience. Two years ago the Dean of Yale College chose that word to differentiate Yale and Stanford in a meeting with a high school student trying to decide between the two. He described Yale's as a healthy intensity, as a passionate pursuit of the things we do. So Yale taught me to pursue my interests and talents vigorously

Balance of work and play–Maintaining a balance of work and play is another lesson I learned at Yale. Keeping that balance was more difficult in graduate school and still more difficult in the face of greater demands in professional life. However, I was determined over the years to keep that balance. I continue to believe that the proper perspective on life requires that you do some things just for the fun of it.

People–I stayed an extra week in New Haven after graduation, walking the streets and visiting old haunts for the last time with a friend or two, feeling stressed out and abandoned and plotting how to stay at Yale somehow for a few more years. One classmate, wiser than I, pointed out the error of my thinking. He said that Yale is no more than a shell for the people we had known and the things we had experienced during our four years. Staying in New Haven wouldn't re-create that. It was time to move on. He was right, of course. It was the quality of the people that counted and would continue to count in the future, if we choose our friends well. Yale taught me the value of good friends and many classmates are good friends today.

Public Service –I remember hearing this advice at Yale: "You've been given a lot and you have an obligation to give something back to society." Yale's tradition of public service was hard to miss and it shaped my thinking about career choices. It wasn't enough just to "do well" if you weren't also "doing good." While I didn't dedicate myself to public service, I made sure I made some contribution to the public good, both professionally and personally.

. . .

Disappointments? Sure, in all areas of life and usually involving not having enough time, not getting enough done, not having enough skills, or not being in the right place at the right time. I view them all as part of the risk-taking I talked about above. With enough areas of interest, when one thing was sagging, usually another was surging, so on balance the disappointments have not been too significant.

What may lie ahead? More of the same, I hope. It's been a great adventure up to now, and I cannot conceive that it won't continue to be. I'm looking forward to pressing on with my work, to getting more light, dry powder, to knowing my children as adult friends. But I confess I'm beginning to become concerned about the passage of time. It's beginning to go faster than it used to. I'm sure it is.

Epilogue

So, well, there you have it. The Yale experience in a nutshell. It's Yale as I have lived it and loved it–perhaps the most formative experience of my life. I have included the quotes from so many people because I wanted you to have reinforcement of my opinions from other parties.

I lived all five of Kingman Brewster's stages of an undergraduate career. I endured the agonies of getting lost and I enjoyed the luxury of finding myself. I explored things for which I had talent, but in which I eventually lost interest, and I explored things in which I was interested, but for which I had no talent.

I have placed the traditions and institutions at Yale in their historical perspective in hopes that the vestiges of those traditions and institutions that remain at Yale will have greater meaning for you.

To paraphrase Dick Brodhead: Women and men of the Yale College Class of the Unforeseeable Future, since you have not yet become Yale students, I have the honor to be your first Yale instructor. I hope I have imparted sufficient knowledge about Yale to allow you to make informed judgments about whether to apply to Yale. I hope you do apply and do make it. It's a great ride.

Oh, and this material *will* be on the exam.